# Cybersecurity for Beginners

The essentials of cybersecurity, cybercrime, cyber-terrorism & hacktivism. What are they? Where are they headed? How do you make cybersecurity work?

# Cybersecurity for Beginners

**Raef Meeuwisse**

Second Edition

Cyber Simplicity Ltd
2015 - 2017

www.cybersimplicity.com

Cyber Simplicity Ltd, 27 Old Gloucester Street, London, UK. WC1N 3AX.

| | |
|---|---|
| Contact us: | www.cybersimplicity.com /contact-us |
| Twitter: | @RaefMeeuwisse |
| First Printing: | May 2015 |
| Second Edition: | March 2017 |
| Edition Date: | 14 March 2017 |
| ISBN | 978-1-911452-03-4 (paperback) |
| | 978-1-911452-13-3 (hardback) |
| | 978-1-911452-15-7 (ebook) |
| Published by: | Cyber Simplicity Ltd |

www.cybersecurityforbeginners.com

www.cybersimplicity.com

Ordering Information:

Special discounts are available on quantity purchases by corporations, associations, educators, and others. For details, contact the publisher at the above listed address.

Trade bookstores and wholesalers: Please contact Cyber Simplicity Ltd.

Tel/Fax: +44(0)1227 540 540 or via www.cybersimplicity.com /contact-us.

# Dedication

For Dawn Meeuwisse, whose passing makes it clear that technology will not replace everything. For Ruth, whose patience has helped me complete the book.

For you the reader. Thank you for buying this book. This is the second edition, please continue to let me know where you want it improved by tweeting me @RaefMeeuwisse.

# Also Available

Also available from this author in paperback & digital formats:

**Cybersecurity Exposed: The Cyber House Rules**
Explores the causes for the increased magnitude and frequency of cybercrime. Why is cybersecurity frequently left vulnerable to attack? Is there a set of principles that can be applied to help correct the problems? A great follow-on read from Cybersecurity for Beginners.

**The Cybersecurity to English Dictionary**
A useful companion for anyone who wants to keep up with cybersecurity terms or confound others with their understanding. Finally, cybersecurity does not need to sound like a different language. An expanded version of the section at the end of this book with hundreds of additional cybersecurity terms defined.

**The Encrypted Pocketbook of Passwords**
Writing down your passwords is usually fraught with risks. The Encrypted Pocketbook of Passwords helps you to store your passwords more securely in a format that you can read but that others will find hard to break.

**Cybersecurity: Home and Small Business**
Guidance on the basic security practices we can apply at home or in small businesses to help decrease the risk of being successfully attacked.

**Cyber with Rosie**
A fun crime, comedy fiction for release in November 2017. When a cybersecurity specialist dies in suspicious circumstances, who is his mysterious replacement and just what is her agenda?

**How to Keep Your Stuff Safe Online**
A low cost microbook providing guidance on the basic security practices we can apply to protect our online devices and the services we subscribe to.

*If you aren’t concerned about Cybersecurity,*

*you don’t know enough about it.*

# Contents

# Chapter Outline

**1: Cybersecurity & Its Origins.**
Describes how reliant we have become on our electronic devices and the reasons that we all need to be concerned about cybersecurity.

**2: About the Case Studies.**
Establishes the format, content and purpose of the case studies and provides some initial terminology definitions.

**3: Case Study: Target 2013.**
Uses facts from the theft of over 40 million customer cardholder details to demonstrate that cybersecurity breaches tend to result from a long list of security gaps.

**4: The Disciplines Within Cybersecurity.**
Begins to introduce the list of skills required to put together a cybersecurity team.

**5: Case Study: Edward Snowden 2013.**
Reinforces the fact that breaches are not due to a single gap. Introduces insider threats and the importance of human factors to cybersecurity.

**6: Basic Cybersecurity Concepts.**
Demonstrates how common sense is still at the core of cybersecurity. Introduces existing, established approaches used to combat threats.

**7: Human Factors.**
Technology does not fail without human involvement. Outlines how and why people are considered the weakest links in the cybersecurity chain.

**8: Technical Factors.**
Looks at the core of current cybersecurity approaches; examines the technical protections typically used to protect against the threats.

**9: Evolving Attack & Defense Methods.**
Reviews how attack and defense methods are evolving.

**10: Case Study: Sony 2014.**
Brings together how human and technical factors can combine to create devastating consequences in a very recent example.

**11. The Cybersecurity Cold War.**
Covers the range of different organizations and individuals that are looking to benefit from cybersecurity gaps and what their motives are.

**12. Risk-Based Cybersecurity & Stacked Risks.**
Increases understanding of how to measure risks more thoroughly and protect against chains of risks forming and failing together.

**13. How Cyber Exposed Are You?**
Provides some simple, logical self-checks to instantly understand how confident you are (or are not) about your organization's cybersecurity status.

**14. What To Do When Things Go Wrong.**
How to manage Security Incidents through a logical process.

**15. A Glimpse Toward the Future.**
Predicts the major technical changes expected over the next 10 years and then looks out as far as 2050 to understand where cybersecurity is headed.

**16. Bringing It All Together.**
Pulls all of the aspects of cybersecurity that have been discussed in the book together to reinforce readers' confidence in understanding cybersecurity, where it fails and how to put effective defenses in place.

**Cybersecurity To English (Definitions)**
An A-to Z list of cybersecurity-related terms in this book.
Note that an expanded version of the Cybersecurity to English Dictionary is available to purchase separately.

*Nobody ever made a statue to honor a committee*

# Preface

This is the second edition of this book. While cybersecurity concerns continue to multiply, there are still very few good introductory books on the subject of cybersecurity. The reasons are simple:

- Most cybersecurity experts get paid too much to write books.
- Most of us are really busy.
- Very few of us know what we are doing well enough to put our reputation on the line by writing a book on the subject.

We also have to keep up to date. The subject area is evolving fast.

As I prepare the second edition, there is still no global consensus on how to write the word 'cybersecurity'. Is it one word or two? In the US, the Department of Homeland Security (DHS), the National Institute of Standards and Technology (NIST) and ISACA (the Information Security Audit and Control Association) use the one word version. So does this book. In the UK, they continue to split the term into two words: cyber security.

After attending multiple information security and cybersecurity conferences each year, often as a speaker, I began to realize in discussions with literally hundreds of professionals just how little concise and reliable information was available in the public domain. As information and cybersecurity professionals constantly try to keep up with what the latest threats are and with how to effectively measure, manage and monitor them, the books and other resources they create tend to be geared toward other IT (information technology) professionals.

But now that technology and digital devices are a core part of any organization and are critical to most people at an individual level, I realized that almost everybody would like to better understand this subject area. Since cybersecurity now affects everyone, I saw a need for basic information that non-technical people would find accessible.

This book explores the *discipline* of cybersecurity and how it should operate in all types of enterprises. If you are only looking for guidance on how to cover personal cybersecurity – try my other publication "**How to Keep Your Stuff Safe Online.**"

My aim was to create something less technical and more informative than other available texts, providing an easy insight into how we got to need cybersecurity, what the implications are and how effective methods of controlling and mitigating the associated problems work.

This book is thus designed to be a one-stop essential text for **anybody** who wants to get a broad, rapid and holistic view of the subject area. You do not need any previous technical knowledge to understand the text. Whenever a technical term is used, you will usually find a plain, non-technical English definition right below its first usage (otherwise - you can always look the term up in the back of the book).

Although I have worked in security and compliance for well over a decade, it was not until 2009 that I began to need to specifically review and audit cybersecurity. I was lucky to be sponsored by one of the largest companies in the world to look into both their internal controls and those required for their most significant suppliers.

One of my early assignments was to prepare a white paper on the capabilities and limitations of Amazon Web Services, Salesforce and other Internet-based platforms. The importance of the sponsoring company and subject matter provided me with access to some of the best cybersecurity minds on the planet and to a rapid and early appreciation of cyber risks and how to mitigate them.

At around the same time, a Fortune 50 company commissioned me to compile their first version of a synchronized set of governance controls that would satisfy all their major global security, privacy and compliance requirements. That required reviewing, organizing, deconstructing and reconstructing over 9,000 controls. The finished library was less than 5% of the size of the original (just under 400 controls) but still met every single relevant requirement.

This exercise in harmonizing controls, coupled with my frequent practical reviews of operational environments, gave me a deep understanding of the known cybersecurity risks and how to mitigate or eliminate them.

Although many of the primary methods of securing technologies have remained the same, the sophistication of attacks is driving a substantial expansion of the security controls available to protect, detect, block, investigate and recover from attempts at unauthorized access.

We are still at the dawn of cybersecurity. There are plenty of poorly defended organizations (and individuals) that continue to be compromised by more knowledgeable adversaries. The speed at which technology is now evolving is going to make that situation worse rather than better. Established companies can easily fall behind if they are unable to safely leverage new technologies. Conversely, more companies you never heard of until recently take their place in the

Fortune 500, FTSE 100 and other listings because they are tech-savvy and focus on safely and more rapidly leveraging and implementing new technologies.

There are also a really large number of cybersecurity jobs on offer around the world – in 2016 experts estimated that about one million such jobs remained unfilled. Nearly all of the organizations that need cybersecurity professionals are struggling to find suitable candidates. The fact is that very few people were working specifically in this sector until about 2013, and the number of qualified professionals has not yet caught up with the demand.

When organizations advertise a role and put in the required section 'Must have at least 10 years cybersecurity experience,' it makes cybersecurity people chuckle. That level of experience rarely exists and is nearly irrelevant when it does. We also do not apply for such jobs unless we are 'fond of a treat' (a British expression of irony suggesting the person enjoys inviting pain and suffering on him or herself). Who wants to take on the challenge of working for an enterprise that lacks even a basic understanding of the modern cybersecurity industry? Nobody wants to be employed only as a scapegoat.

During the next few years, we will regularly (almost daily at present) see some truly spectacular stories hit the mainstream press about the next organization that got caught with gaps in their cybersecurity defenses. Since I wrote the first edition of this book, these breaches have included millions of personal details stolen from the US Office of Personnel Management and a billion account details from Yahoo. So how is this happening?

It is happening because, like anything new, we are not yet mature and stable at using our digital devices. If you imagine how things were in the early days of the car, there was no clear idea about where to locate the steering wheel, so it started out being in the center of the car on many models. There were no seatbelts, roll cages or airbags. People were just amazed that the car moved without a horse strapped to the front, so they started out calling it 'The Horseless Carriage.'

The current digital era is very much like those early days of the car. It is the wild west of technology out there right now. A new gold rush. Companies are often unknowingly staking everything on each new technology they connect to their digital ecosystem.

The speed and budget that most of us still apply to adopting new technology is often a risk-based gamble. This book will help you to better understand those risks and how to control them. Use the right new technologies quickly and you can benefit greatly. Spend time and money on verifying technology and its security before you use it and you will be safer, but you could fall behind your competition.

So if you really want to understand the discipline of cybersecurity, including its risks and how to control them, read on.

# Introduction

"If you are not concerned about cybersecurity, you don't know enough about it."

I thought those words were just another attempt at fear-based selling - until I immersed myself in the subject and saw that blind faith in digital devices was accelerating past the security skills of most people and organizations that use them.

The lure of lower costs and higher earnings encourages us all to adopt new technologies very quickly. Do we understand the risks? Do we **want** to understand the risks? Do we know anybody who can actually tell us what the risks really are?

Did you ever download a free software application? Did you ever consider that this application was not free - the price was access to information on your phone, tablet or computer?

If you want to understand the risks in plain English, without technical clutter, this book is for you. It will give you a broad insight into where we are, how we got here, where we are headed and how to take effective steps at a personal and organizational level to ensure you are better protected.

The book is designed to form an integrated, comprehensive story arc. You will derive the most benefit from it if you choose to read it from cover to cover. If you want to take a more fragmented approach, each chapter is also designed to be self-contained and can be read without knowledge from the preceding chapters.

There is also a short, abridged Cybersecurity to English dictionary at the back of this book that allows you to look up key technical terms used in cybersecurity and to obtain a translation into everyday English.

The subject of cybersecurity is incredibly relevant to us all, and not understanding it poses personal and professional risks. This book provides fast access and understanding to anyone who wants to know about this subject area.

People tend to prefer concise, fact-based content, so this book is built to deliver that punchy format.

Whether you are a business person, politician, everyday human (perhaps one who has lost data) or existing security specialist who is looking to update your knowledge, this book will raise your eyebrows and enhance your knowledge of this fascinating and dangerous subject area.

# 1. Cybersecurity & Its Origins

We are living through the most significant period of change that has ever taken place in human history – the digital revolution.

If you could travel back in time just 30 years, you would be living in a world where if all the computers and electronics were shut off, everyone and everything, including the products and services we rely on, would be able to function and recover without catastrophe.

That is no longer true.

If someone were able to switch every digital and electronic device off today, planes would drop out of the sky, cars would stop working, supermarkets would close, large companies would not know who worked for them and most banks would probably have no idea about who owed who what.

There is even a phenomenon that can switch off all these devices. It is called an electromagnetic pulse, or EMP.

Any electronic device exposed to an EMP will end up with every single component destroyed. These pulses are highly unlikely to occur naturally, but can be created artificially and actually comprise the working parts of some man-made weaponry. However, aside from people in the military, nobody used to worry too much about the potential risk of an EMP.

They do now.

Most major organizations now regularly place a copy of their most critical data in an EMP pulse-proof environment known as a Faraday cage, or place copies of their critical information in far off locations.

You might think that to a greater or lesser extent, you have opted out of an over-reliance on the digital age, but there is almost no service or product that you use that is not fully dependent on technology.

Hospitals, transport vehicles, shops, the electricity and water in your house, and pretty much every product and service in everyday life will stop working if the technology they now rely upon stops functioning.

You are almost certainly reliant on the cyber world in ways that regularly, if not constantly, put your life in the hands of technology.

The rate of change we are experiencing is also not slowing down; it is actually accelerating.

Human activities and behaviors have changed more in the past 10 years than they did in any 10 year period in all of human history. One source of evidence for this point comes from an example used by different speakers at several presentations I attended:

> *There are two photographs that involve the selection of two Popes.*
>
> *In the first photo, taken in 2005, a large crowd of people are standing in Vatican City watching as white smoke appears to announce the selection of the new Pope, Benedict.*
>
> *Just eight years later, a photo taken from exactly the same spot relates to the selection of Pope Francis on March 13, 2013. There are similar numbers of people in the crowd, but this time all that can be seen is a sea of illuminated screens showing smartphones and tablets in almost every single person's hand - periscopes up, hands held high to capture the images.*

If you take a look around you at any coffee shop, train station, or airport, you will notice a lot of people engaging with some or other device; smartphones, tablets and headsets are now ubiquitous. And yet the very first iPhone (arguably the first smart device to catch on in a huge way), was only released in 2007.

In the UK, an Ofcom report in 2014 found that the average UK adult spent more time using electronic devices than they did sleeping:

- 8 hours 41 minutes per day using or viewing some type of ***digital device***.
- 8 hours 21 minutes per day sleeping.

The simple truth is that if you use digital devices effectively, they make you more powerful. They can make you richer, save you money, boost your quality of life, better entertain you and improve your social connections.

But are these technologies 100% secure, safe and reliable? These are not questions that most of us usually bother to contemplate unless or until we are hit by a problem.

As mentioned in the introduction, the lure of lower costs, higher earnings and more immediate fun encourages most of us to adopt new technologies very quickly. But do we understand the risks? Do we ***want*** to understand the risks? Do we know anybody who can actually tell us what the risks really are?

Whenever you download a 'free' application, it is certain there is a price being paid. Even the most humble game or flashlight application is almost definitely taking information about you, including your location and your device ID, and probably your phone number, phone contacts and a lot more. Some mainstream applications actually have permission to monitor your phone calls and emails (although whether they use the permission is still often unknown and remains a fuzzy area of debate).

Perhaps you are feeling smug and have never downloaded such an app? Well, if you have a smartphone, tablet or laptop, the chances are almost certain that the device manufacturer or service provider already loaded a few applications and slipped those permissions into your agreement with them.

Consider the Windows 10 operating system. The initial release came bundled with software and default permissions to monitor your web behavior, offer ads based on your known preferences, and even to use your own machine and network bandwidth to help distribute Microsoft updates to other machines on the Internet.

We live in an age in which collecting information is power.

Organizations collect information to build their power. They want to learn how to improve their products and services. They collect customer information to better target their customers and improve sales. They collect data on their competitors to understand threats and opportunities. They also collect information to sell to other companies.

But what happens when an unauthorized person or organization can get hold of someone else's cache of their most sensitive and valuable information?

Do you remember the humiliation that a child would have to endure when some mean kid, or intrusive parent, got hold of his or her diary? Well, let's magnify that to a corporate scale. We saw the consequences in April 2016 at Mossack Fonseca (a Panamanian law firm that delivers services including helping wealthy people make efficient offshore investments) and in December 2014 with Sony when their private corporate emails were leaked. We will also look at the Sony breach as a case study later on in the book.

It is tempting to think that ***cybersecurity*** is only about people trying to ***hack*** and steal other peoples' information. Indeed, most cybersecurity efforts are focused on protecting digital devices and their information from the continual barrage of digital attacks that occur. Cybersecurity certainly includes those measures, but is also a much wider and more significant discipline, in part because the people trying to gain unauthorized access often have motives other than stealing information or money.

For example, in January 2015, the social media accounts of the US military Central Command (CENTCOM) were accessed by attackers claiming allegiance to the Islamic State. Their intention was not to steal data, but to take control of a communication channel and manipulate it. The motivation was not financial; instead their aim was to create a profile for their cause and unrest within their enemy.

This is a good place to precisely define what cybersecurity is.

***cybersecurity**** *– the protection of* ***digital devices*** *and their communication channels to keep them stable, dependable and reasonably safe from danger or threat. Usually the required protection level must be sufficient to prevent or address* ***unauthorized access*** *or intervention before it can lead to substantial personal, professional, organizational, financial and/or political harm.*

***digital device*** *– any electronic appliance that can create, modify, archive, retrieve or transmit information in an electronic format. Desktop computers, laptops, tablets, smartphones and Internet-connected home devices are all examples of digital devices.*

*NOTE: For any term that appears in* ***bold italic text****, a definition can also be found in* ***The Cybersecurity to English*** *section at the end of the book.*

**The asterisk after a term denotes that a fuller definition of this term is available at the back of the book.*

Despite the fact that cybersecurity is front and center in today's world, when I was conducting part of my research for this book (early 2015), I was shocked to discover that even Wikipedia had not yet allowed a specific entry for the term 'cybersecurity' to be created – it just re-directed to 'Computer Security.'

This delay in promoting widespread knowledge about cybersecurity is at least partly attributable to the speed at which cybersecurity has gained prominence and continues to evolve. Just a few short years after the need for cybersecurity became apparent, industry professionals are now aware that this discipline is about protecting a lot more than computers. In fact, it is about more than protecting any and all technologies. Cybersecurity is really about protecting people, who, directly or indirectly, rely on anything electronic.

It is now becoming accepted that cybersecurity also encompasses the need to keep electronic devices and digital services stable and dependable. Specifically, following a cybersecurity strategy that relies on prevention alone no longer works. It is necessary for modern organizations to also have the ability to detect unexpected or unauthorized disruptions, and to then quickly diagnose the issues and resolve, address and then restore the affected services.

Most early cybersecurity efforts focused primarily on protection against malicious and intentional threats to technology. However, it is now accepted that systems can be taken out of action because of process gaps, unexpected user actions, and even rogue insider activities, just as easily as they can through external malicious attacks. For example, in February 2017, Amazon Web Services suffered a partial service outage due to a very minor typo by an employee who was trying to debug the billing system. That outage took popular services such as Netflix, Tinder, Airbnb, Reddit and IMDb offline for several hours.

The US National Security Agency (NSA) and their ***Defense in Depth*** strategy documents have helped expert audiences appreciate the wider threats, including human factors. There is even an entire chapter dedicated to human factors. The NSA's issues with Edward Snowden highlighted how people are still usually the weakest link in the cybersecurity chain.

***defense in depth*** *- the use of multiple layers of security techniques to help reduce the chance of a successful attack. The idea is that if one security technique fails or is bypassed, there are others that should address the attack. The latest (and correct) thinking on defense in depth is that security techniques must also consider people and operations (for example processes) factors and not just technology.*

Guarding against external and malicious threats is considered a priority because they currently appear to create the most damage and cost. This is because most (but not all) major cybersecurity incidents are due to criminal, state or terrorist-led activities. Even the threats from insiders tend to create the most impact when they are either (i) intentional, or (ii) when they are targeted to serve as an access point to an environment.

A malicious attack often includes the unauthorized removal or copying of information. These information leaks often cause customer, brand and share damage in addition to high remediation and compensation costs.

A system outage can also create these costs, but they are usually at a different and lower scale. There are occasional exceptions. A UK air traffic control system outage in December 2015 and other similar events can be caused simply by deploying inadequately tested updates to software.

So how has it happened that in recent years, we passed our lives into the hands of digital devices?

Back in 1990, I got my first mobile phone. I was at University, and the line rental cost about the equivalent of 1 week's room rent. The phone was the size of half a house brick and weighed about the same. Calls were so expensive that only the most desperate to talk would call. The reception was so bad that you had to be somewhere in an urban center to make or receive calls. I would get comments about how pointless it was to have a mobile phone. Even by the late 90's many people were still stating that they would never buy or own a mobile phone. Then it became so cheap, mainstream and disadvantageous not to have one – that almost everyone now does.

In 1995, I first connected to the Internet. My early Internet connection was not dissimilar to the early days of the mobile phone. The connection speed was tens of thousands of times slower than it is today. It cost a fortune to connect (charged by the minute) and the speed was so slow that even loading a simple text-based web page could take several minutes. Downloading a simple program could take hours or days.

The services available on the early Internet were so basic and slow that there was little information of monetizable value for anyone to try to attack. There were enough ***virus***es around to create problems for these early users, especially if they did not take the step of installing anti-virus software. However, the slow connection speeds meant that you really had to try hard, visit some pretty dubious sites and avoid installing anti-virus software to be at risk. Even then, the maximum risk was usually just the time and expense of re-installing your computer files.

***virus*** *– a form of malicious software that spreads by infecting (attaching itself) to other files and usually seeks opportunities to continue that pattern. Viruses are now less common than other forms of* **malware***. Viruses were the main type of malware in very early computing. For that reason, people often refer to some-*

*thing as a virus when it is technically another form of malware.*

The transformation that gave rise to cybersecurity threats was mostly driven by one key factor: Internet connection speeds became faster, cheaper and more widely adopted, even in less economically developed countries.

This change, together with faster computer processing speeds and better web application programming, gradually made it easier, more effective and cheaper to provide mainstream services through the Internet, rather than using traditional offline routes. Activities like banking, shopping, watching movies and listening to broadcasts became more convenient online.

Until very recently, there were still organizations and people that could thrive and survive without using Internet-connected devices.

But as the digital connection speeds and service options derived from using 'connected' technologies grew, those people and organizations that chose to leverage connected devices found that these devices provided significant advantages. They were paying less, incurring lower costs, earning more and even socializing more.

As more organizations and people adopted connected technologies, traditional (disconnected) services became even less competitive due to their higher costs and lower benefits.

This created a 'Darwin' effect. Those who adapted to the advantages of connected technologies were (and are) gaining advantages and thriving. Those organizations that were (and are) not evolving to use connected technologies are mostly shrinking or perishing.

A connected person can find all sorts of financial and social opportunities. Any person who is not connected to the Internet is paying more and experiencing fewer opportunities.

Organizations find themselves in a similar position. If they do not fully leverage the advantages of interconnected technologies, they have fewer opportunities than others that do.

All of this resulted in people and organizations placing much more information of monetizable value into their 'connected' electronic devices, together with connection speeds that allow the information to quickly flow in and out of these devices.

We now routinely store and transact very sensitive information and services through networked devices. Our credit card details and medical information are online, and we even use the Internet as a primary method of correspondence. This means there is substantial information about us in our connected devices.

It is also important to remember that even the very first electronic computers were used for breaking into information, or, more accurately, code breaking through the use of ***cryptanalysis***.

***cryptanalysis*** *- the art of examining* ***ciphered*** *information to determine how to circumvent the technique that was used to encode or hide it. Analyzing ciphers.*

The work of Alan Turing and others during the second world war used the very first forms of electronic computing to help break the Nazi enigma code (used for German secret communications), and is widely believed to be a key contributor to the allies winning the war.

Opinion varies on when the first computer attacks took place, but it should be clear that for as long as humans have used computing power, it has been used to both enhance how we use our own information and to take advantages away from competitors.

Even my own school network of computers had a virus written by a very computer-savvy friend of mine back in 1985. This virus insisted that people 'have a cookie' before they could proceed with their real work.

However, the large-scale threats and thefts took a lot longer to gain public visibility. There were occasional scare stories of clever programmers in the 80s and 90s taking money by subverting computer programs in (for example) a few large banks.

But it was not until around 2005 that most organizations (and people) began to allow high-value content to move in and out of their secure networks, even though these organizations and people used computers extensively for many decades before this.

Until around 2005, nearly all IT (information technology) departments controlled which devices and software could be used in any organization. 'Technology' was typically a partially effective department, with a reputation for being full of geeks who selected and rolled out systems that were frequently (but not always) of little or no business value. At that time, with the exception of some permitted web browsing, technologies used by organizations operated nearly exclusively inside a protected internal network as well.

For the average technology department, releasing products that were stable, secure and worked well was often a higher priority than understanding the actual business needs of the people or organizations for which these products were intended.

It was not that these geek-controlled departments didn't care; instead, most companies' policies resulted in the placement of technology-oriented people, rather than those with business and communication skills, in leadership positions.

Organizations tended to promote introverted programmers, who struggled with social interaction, into project, program and senior technology managers. These managers were then put in contact with business units which had limited commercial knowledge, and everyone was surprised that these technology managers were terrible at communicating and kept building things for technical satisfaction rather than for the business purposes that executives envisioned, but perhaps could not describe.

Organizations also allowed these departments to operate and deliver with the speed of a tazered snail in winter. I came into technology from a field where 'I will get right on it' meant that you would get something done in the next few minutes. In the technology arena, one often struggled to get any technology department to put an accurate year against a delivery date.

Whatever the failings of these internal IT departments, they did tend to be very good at keeping their organizations' technologies safe. After all, if they had messed up in a big way, their careers might have been on the line. So they followed a very narrow, set process of keeping information and technologies inside a restricted and protected perimeter.

At that time, the other major challenges for IT departments included:

- In large companies, nearly everything was custom-made. Businesses would ask their technology departments to build software from a clean page, often based on very limited business knowledge of what we needed.
- Smaller companies often could not afford the software for some tasks. They just managed with manual processes or by using local spreadsheets or databases.

Then, with the enhanced connection speeds of the Internet, the ***cloud*** arrived.

**cloud* (the)** - *An umbrella term used to identify any technology service that uses software and equipment not physically managed or developed by the person or organization (customer) using it. This usually provides advantages of on-demand scalability at lower cost. Examples include* **applications** *that are hosted online, online file storage areas, even providing remote virtual computers. Using a cloud will mean the equipment managing the service is run by the cloud provider and not the customer. Usually a cloud service is indicated by an 'aaS' suffix. For example -* **SaaS** *(Software as a Service),* **IaaS** *(Infrastructure as a Service) and* **PaaS** *(Platform as a Service).*

The cloud opened up a market for software that offered choices and prices never seen before. Instead of paying thousands or millions for a piece of software, waiting months or years for it to arrive, and then spending more money again to get it 'hosted' (installed on computers), we could all pay a much lower price (sometimes even free) and try out software within a matter of minutes.

This major change in thinking was largely popularized by Apple, their iPhone and their App Store. The App Store opened the eyes of everyday people to the value of being willing to share a platform with other people.

It soon became apparent to company decision-makers (often outside the technology department) that if they applied a similar philosophy to their corporate software, they would have more choices, greater flexibility, and lower costs, especially if they also let the software producer host and manage updates to their products.

The digital revolution was coming of age.

Commercial software (shrink wrapped, self-installed) had been around for decades. However, the time and cost required to purchase and set up the software was usually a barrier for people who wished to try out several alternatives.

The ability to use online software had also been around for some time. For example, we have all been using search engines since the Internet became available. Even salesforce.com started as early as 1999 (Google was only founded in 1998). The big change occurred when the adoption of software that was created, hosted, and even remotely serviced by external companies reached a tipping point. No company could afford to be left behind.

Early cloud adopters were able to significantly outpace their competition, stripping back costs and more importantly, connecting more effectively with their customers.

The risks that some IT experts warned would result from using this software failed to materialize early on in any meaningful way. Indeed, most people found that using cloud software was actually a lot better, cheaper, and faster and even provided a more reliable experience.

Any person or business could now find and choose software that suited their real needs, download it and try it in a matter of minutes. In addition, the software itself was superior to software that was previously created in-house because it was built using a more diverse range of business expertise than had ever been available in any single company.

These cloud opportunities took most of the decisions about technology choices away from IT departments, but left them with the responsibility of securing these externally-administered tools after the decision was made. The decision-making power in most companies now lies with non-IT personnel, and when it comes to selecting any technology or software that can create revenue or lower operating costs, the technology department is now just a consultancy service.

Technology departments no longer dictate which software their company will use; instead, business executives tell the IT department what it needs to integrate and support for the benefit of the entire company. It has become increasingly important for personnel who understand their company's business needs to make these decisions to keep pace with the competition. Everyone associated with a particular company is thus obligated to adopt new technologies that can drive up the value of the company's products or services.

This has profoundly changed the role and skills requirements of technology departments. Any information security person who stopped working in 2009 and came back to the field today would barely recognize the functions of the IT or cybersecurity departments.

The hard truth is that the technology landscape has changed so much in the past 10 years that a significant number of people who work in the field don't really understand current technologies. Even a good technologist who keeps up to date will have to step back to research and re-train him or herself before answering specific questions about totally new technologies.

(Whenever I make this point in speeches I give at conferences, I see a wave of nodding heads that signify my colleagues' agreement.)

However, this does not mean that the role of technologists has diminished; in fact, technology departments have progressed from playing a peripheral role to being the critical foundation upon which each and every organization on the planet relies.

Cybersecurity experts who now sit at the top of certain government organizations and cyber communities confidently predict that it will be routine for a ***Chief Information Security Officer*** (***CISO***) or a CISO equivalent to hold a position on all major organizations' executive boards before the end of 2018. Cybersecurity departments led by a CISO now play a central role in controlling the destiny of these organizations and their leaders because after all, there are only 2 ways any CEO can unwillingly lose his or her job: (i) poor share price performance or (ii) a massive loss of sensitive information that evidence determines was due to substantial gaps in the organization's cybersecurity. Only item (ii) seems to happen overnight.

The primary role of a modern 'business technology' department is to establish and manage methods by which an organization can work smoothly and securely with a combination of in-house and external technologies. To do this, the department leaders must establish a centralized security architecture and must work with each internal and external supplier to establish roles, responsibilities, boundaries, standards and other ***controls***.

To put this more simply, it is very much like a set of scales. Unless the convenience and money-saving advantages of using externally-supplied technologies are balanced with comparable investments in security, bad things can happen. Companies and individuals saved money by choosing to use other peoples' software, but ended up having to invest money to restore an acceptable level of security, stability and technology integration. When this investment is not made, potential vulnerabilities that can contribute to or cause cybersecurity breaches are created.

However, convincing decision-makers that it is important to counterbalance new technologies with investments in security has not been, and still is not, an easily-negotiated process. Here is an example of how early conversations about securing new technologies would run:

<u>Customer Group:</u> We got this great new deal with a provider. They offered to analyze a copy of our most sensitive information. We would like to get some idea of how much it will cost to approve all of the security arrangements?

Tech Department: (After analysis) It will probably cost about $11,000 to check the security and as a ballpark, based on information already available, perhaps at least an additional $30,000 to put the additional security required in place.

Customer Group: (Does the face). That's ridiculous; we are only paying $2,000 for their service for the first year.

Tech Department: Yes, but you are placing a copy of data worth at least tens of millions of dollars with them... (and maybe the reason the price is so low is that they want access to your data, so they can use and resell it in some way...)

The disconnect between the ways in which people in the customer group and tech departments view the value of security stems from 3 basic factors:

- Information is valuable
- Risks cost money to control
- Until an organization gets hit by a substantial risk, it is tempted to save money by being as minimalist as possible with its controls.

These risks are not just from external suppliers. Any digital device that is used directly or indirectly to help us run our lives and businesses is a potential point of ***vulnerability***.

In the cybersecurity world, any potential vulnerability that might be leveraged is called an attack ***vector***.

***vulnerability**** *– (in the context of **cybersecurity**) a weakness that could be compromised and result in damage or harm.*

***vector*** *– another word for 'method' – as in 'They used multiple vectors for the attack.'*

The more variety we have in what we allow in our selection of digital devices and the software that sits on them, the more potential vulnerabilities and vectors we have.

Consider mobile email as an example. For a time, Blackberry was the market's leading choice for many organizations when it came to mobile email. Many organizations procured and provided these specific devices to help control their employees' use of them. As an employee entitled to mobile email, you potentially had 2 choices:

1) Have mobile email and a Blackberry or
2) Don't have mobile email and have whatever phone you like.

In that scenario, cybersecurity was easier. There was only one set of vectors to worry about.

Now consider the trend of 'Bring Your Own Device' (***BYOD***) to work. This is a common policy in which companies allow their employees to purchase any phone or tablet from anywhere and to then use it for company-related work, potentially including corporate email. How do you make that secure? If you have really large pockets, there are ways to mitigate this danger, but without doubt the associated security costs start to exceed the value and convenience of the devices. For that reason, many companies that initially adopted BYOD have reverted to restricting the range and configuration of devices that can be used to handle corporate information.

Regardless of the potential threats, many companies do allow employees and some contractors to use their own personal equipment inside their network and/or to access privileged or sensitive information. It is no coincidence that the uptake of BYOD tends to be higher in poorer countries with more relaxed attitudes towards the safety of company information.

Organizations have never lived as dangerously as they do right now. Everybody has heard of 'cutting edge' technology. This is a term used to describe the latest and most desirable innovations. But today many organizations and individuals are using ***'bleeding edge'*** technologies.

***bleeding edge*** *– using inventions so new, they have the likelihood to cause damage to their population before they become stable and safe.*

BYOD is an example of bleeding edge technology usage.

In the battle to lower costs and raise earnings, the uptake of bleeding edge opportunities, even by major global companies, has sometimes been astoundingly short-sighted. In simple terms, the immediate business value of a technology or device is often presented and decided upon in isolation, without an accurate understanding of the wider security and stability risks to the organization.

For example – the business case benefit for BYOD is often presented as the perception that having employees purchase their own devices saves the company money and increases employee productivity because many employees seem to be more comfortable using their own devices for both personal and work-related tasks. On the other side of the equation, there are billions of combinations of free applications and software that can be loaded onto peoples' personal devices. This means there are more vulnerability combinations (vectors again) than can possibly be considered or mitigated.

BYOD will become stable and will work in a few years, but we have yet to fully develop the necessary controls and safety mechanisms at this point in time. For every expert who suggests a new solution to secure peoples' personal devices, I can find 4 or 5 other experts who propose different ways of defeating the proposed protection. That is a clear indicator of a substantial and ongoing risk.

It can also be argued that the risk from the vulnerability presented by a single mobile device is too small to be a concern. After all, what can ***hackers*** steal from a single device that is connected to a cyber network?

What we have above is an example of a risk that is only being partially considered. These small individual risks are the type that can, and do, come together (see Chapter 12 on 'Stacked Risks') to precipitate what is commonly referred to as a major cybersecurity breach. Or, as the UK's Information Commissioner's Office (ICO) referred to its own loss in 2014 – a 'non-trivial data breach.'

Having control over (i) access to your digital devices and to the (ii) information they store and transact are two of the most important elements in cybersecurity.

If you need a device to be fully secure, it really is as simple as considering electronic information in a digital device to be no different than water in a container. You do not want the water to leak out; you only want to be able to pour it out when you want it poured. The same thing applies to any digital device. The more holes you (and others) punch for pouring, the more likely it is that the device will spring a leak.

Just like in plumbing systems, you also have to worry about access, leaks and weaknesses wherever you allow your information to flow. The more variety and options in your cyber-plumbing, the harder it will be to keep it secure.

When you think about how extensive the cyber-plumbing for a large organization can be, you begin to understand the enormous difficulties involved in achieving and sustaining a secure environment. For that very reason, organizations often have different security 'zones,' with the highest level of security applied only to the places that hold and transact the most sensitive information.

Consider, for example, the flight control system of a modern plane. It is run by a computer, but is also designed to be completely enclosed. If you use an electronic device on a plane that provides an Internet connection, this uses a completely different system than the flight controls do. The only possible connection they share is using the plane's power system. Or at least that was what I thought until 2015.

I am a private pilot myself, so was interested in an article about a patent for which Boeing applied in 2003. Something they call the Boeing Honeywell Uninterruptable Autopilot (BHUAP). It is essentially an anti-hijack system that can remove all power and control from the flight deck, with the aircraft still able to operate and fly. Its patent can be found in public records.

In a situation where the BHUAP detects a significant deviation from the expected flight parameters, the system can essentially transfer control of the plane from the pilots and defer to either a pre-programmed emergency flight plan, or it can open a radio frequency link through a piece of standard aircraft equipment called a 'Mode S Transponder' to accept remote flight management.

Perhaps you think these systems are going to be installed sometime in the future? Perhaps they are in place already? Maybe you think that the people testing these systems will be able to consider every possible scenario and failsafe? Mystery surrounds BHUAP, but one thing is perfectly clear – the capacity for remote flight management opens the door to the wrong people gaining control.

Since the first edition of this book was published, there have also been some successful demonstrations of aircraft control systems being accessible through the onboard entertainment systems.

These facts, and similar ones that apply to other digital systems, should give you some preliminary insight into what cybersecurity is and the reasons it has become so important... and a source of stress for many cybersecurity professionals.

Do you sleep soundly at night?

There are very few people who work in the field of cybersecurity who do.

That's because we know most organizations' and individuals' adoption and reliance on technology substantially outpaces their general ability to keep it completely safe and secure.

Cybersecurity would not matter to you or to me if the damage from other peoples' technology choices only damaged these individuals. Unfortunately, the damage extends far beyond those who should be responsible for protecting these technologies.

Growth and power opportunities have encouraged organizations and people, even those in critical product and service areas, to adopt and rely on an ecosystem of digital devices that are often only partially under their own control.

Each time there is a brand new type of vulnerability or method of attack uncovered, you can often still smell the paint drying on the ***controls*** used to mitigate the problem.

***control**** *- (in the context of security and compliance) a method of regulating something, often a process or behavior, to achieve a desired outcome, usually resulting in a reduction of* ***risk.***

Before we look more deeply into current cybersecurity concepts and practices, now would be a good time to look at what kinds of things occur to create a cybersecurity breach.

Keep in mind that cybersecurity is still about humans attacking humans. The only difference between cybersecurity and traditional methods of preventing attacks is that the weapons used to hurt us are our digital devices and the sensitive information they contain.

One of the most profound changes since the first edition of this book was released is the huge boom in the cybercrime industry. Since cybersecurity is generally very poorly managed, many environments, even those that exist in major organizations, often have enough gaps in their defenses that criminals can easily exploit these deficiencies.

The cybercrime industry is now generating hundreds of billions of dollars of revenue each year. Let's look at some case studies of real-life cybersecurity incidents and which factors allowed them to happen.

**cyber insecurity** – *suffering from a concern that weaknesses in your* **cybersecurity** *are going to cause you personal or professional harm.*

# 2. About the Case Studies

In this chapter, we will be looking at our first example of a cybersecurity intrusion, together with some of the key information that was made available about the event.

In each of the case studies, I have used a standard format to help make the incidents easier to review and compare. The content in each case study is based on information that is freely available in the public domain.

From around 2007 until 2013, many industry insiders believed the risks of quickly adopting new technologies were outweighed by the benefits and/or earnings they returned. Even government agencies were caught being complacent about their security posture. Now they are not being as complacent, but they are still being caught out.

A huge issue is just how much happens outside of any enterprise's direct control, but still inside their realm of accountability. As we covered in the last chapter, the flow of information through and onto digital devices is similar to the flow of water through a plumbing system.

As enterprises began to use more and more suppliers, they essentially started attaching their plumbing systems to a lot of other plumbing systems that they did not directly maintain and that they often had not checked for security weaknesses.

Thus, in the race to outsource anything that was not considered absolutely core to each enterprise's operations, information no longer remained in a closed and controlled environment.

Since many cybersecurity weaknesses result from these outsourced connections, whenever I am tasked with auditing a new environment, I look at where the information flows to identify what needs to be audited. Not just the devices and their paths; also the human processes involved in building, delivering, managing and using these devices.

Not all cybersecurity risks come from suppliers; however, suppliers are an example of how, when looking to reduce costs or increase earnings, people can be more inclined to introduce potential new risks.

Each unknown or unmitigated risk opens up vulnerabilities that can become targets for cybersecurity breaches.

As more and more enterprises started losing brand credibility because of very public technology failures, everybody began taking the risks more seriously.

The moment that really changed mainstream corporate board thinking was in late 2013, when Target (the US retailer) discovered that a copy of over 40 million customer details, including credit card numbers, had been stolen. This shift was further compounded in 2014 when Home Depot (another major US retailer) fell victim to a very similar event.

There had been massive data breaches before (and since) the Target event; however, this was the first that had the public visibility, financial scale and overall corporate damage impact that some cybersecurity experts had long predicted.

The moment that really transformed major governments' investments in cybersecurity also occurred in 2013, when a rogue contractor named Edward Snowden disclosed the contents of over a million classified documents. During the time Snowden procured these documents, he did not work directly for the NSA; he worked for a sub-contractor. We will look at that case study later on.

In each of these case studies, these organizations' transparency over the root causes of their issues helps us to understand how problems arise and how to address them.

These incidents also illuminate the fact that a cybersecurity representative from an organization that has suffered a major, well-publicized, breach is likely to be more aware of cybersecurity risks and countermeasures than a counterpart in a company that has never been hit.

Organizations hit by major, public breaches are far less prone to attacks in the future, once they have assessed and addressed their vulnerabilities. Until 2014, most enterprises only invested reactively, after they fell victim to one or more major incidents. But that has changed as a result of these events.

Although the largest cybersecurity incidents receive the most publicity, there are literally tens of thousands of materially substantial events each day. Major enterprises' networks are subject to millions of minor, opportunistic, gap-sensing events every hour.

The case studies in this book have been selected because they are widely-known throughout the world and demonstrate a good mix of the potential causes of damage that arises from having unidentified and/or unmitigated risks. The individual root causes often seem to pose minor risks when looked at in isolation, but when a few of these individual risks are joined together in a line, they have the power to severely damage an organization.

For Target, it was not just one thing that went wrong. In fact, in all the case studies we will look at, you will see that a number of what are referred to as 'control failures' existed and compounded each other to cause the breaches. I call this a 'stacked control failure' as a result of unmitigated 'stacked risks' and have dedicated a chapter to it later in the book.

More recent megabreaches, including Mossack Fonseca in April 2016, Myspace in May 2016, and then Yahoo, continue to demonstrate that the largest compromises stem from multiple gaps in the security defenses. It is difficult to sneak away with several hundred million readily decryptable passwords if all of your security controls are adequate.

Before we look at the Target case study, to understand what happened, we need to define a few more cybersecurity-related terms:

***hacker**** *– a person who engages in attempts to gain* ***unauthorized access*** *to one or more* ***digital devices.***

***cyber attack*** *– to take aggressive or hostile action by leveraging or targeting* ***digital devices.*** *The intended damage is not limited to the digital (electronic) environment.*

Man-made devices and software do not attack each other through their own free will. Behind any ***cyber attack*** there are people, looking to take advantage of any gaps in the defenses. These people may or may not be ***hackers*** themselves, but will certainly engage this type of expertise as part of their offensive.

The primary purpose of any cyber attack is to achieve a monetary and/or political power advantage. Hackers and digital devices are only some of the weaponry used. The basics of any cyber attack can therefore be summarized as follows:

Hostile parties (***threat actors***)

seek

vulnerabilities (security gaps)

to

***exploit*** (take advantage of)

for

financial or political gain.

***exploit*** *– to take advantage of a security* ***vulnerability****. Well-known exploits are often given names. Falling victim to a known exploit with a name can be a sign of low security, such as poor* ***patch management****.*

***threat actors*** *– an umbrella term to describe the collection of people and organizations that work to create* ***cyber attacks****. Examples of threat actors can include* ***cyber criminals, hacktivists*** *and nation states.*

***patch management*** *– a controlled process used to deploy critical, interim updates to software on* ***digital devices****. The release of a software 'patch' is usually in response to a critical flaw or gap that has been identified. Any failure to apply new interim software updates promptly can leave open security* ***vulnerabilities*** *in place. As a consequence, promptly applying these updates (patch management) is considered a critical component of maintaining effective* ***cybersecurity****.*

If or when somebody gets inside your digital devices, the disruption he or she causes and/or the information he or she steals are only secondary to the end goal. The real objective is for the attacker to steal money or to achieve leverage through the theft or through destroying the victim's property.

For example, when credit card data is stolen, this does not create instant money for the thieves (***cyber criminals***) who stole it. The information has to be sold for the attack to be profitable to the perpetrators. The theft is not the endgame; the resale and receipt of cash for the information is.

If someone breaks into your car and steals an item from inside, the cost of repairing the damage caused by the theft can often be much greater than the value of the item stolen. The same is true in the cyber world. The attackers are only interested in their own profit and costs. The only time they are interested in your costs is when they are intentionally aiming to create high costs for you in order to perform some kind of ransom or extortion.

There are also recent examples of physical destruction as a direct result of cyber attacks. For example, in January 2015, Wired (a leading website technology news publication) reported on a cyber attack on a German steel mill that resulted in the inability to shut down the blast furnace and subsequent damage.

*http://www.wired.com/2015/01/german-steel-mill-hack-destruction/*

The tools used by hackers to launch cyber attacks include something called ***malware***.

***malware**** *– shortened version of* ***malicious software****. A term used to describe the insertion of disruptive, subversive or hostile programs onto a* ***digital device****. These types of programs can be intentional or unintentional. Intentional versions are usually disguised or embedded in a file that looks harmless. There are many types of malware;* ***adware, botnets****, computer* ***viruses, ransomware, scareware, spyware, trojans*** *and* ***worms*** *are all examples of intentional malware.* ***Hackers*** *often use malware to mount* ***cybersecurity*** *attacks.*

***botnet*** *– shortened version of* ***robotic network****. A connected set of programs designed to operate together over a* ***network*** *(including the Internet) to achieve specific purposes. The purpose can be good or bad. Some programs of this type are used to help support Internet connections; malicious uses include taking over control of some or all of a computer's functions to support large-scale service attacks (see* ***denial of service****). Botnets are sometimes referred to as a* ***zombie army****.*

However, not all cybersecurity issues are about external threats or internal technical shortcomings. Through the descriptions of the case studies, you will notice that all cybersecurity breaches have a very strong human component.

Humans control all digital devices and the processes used to design, build, operate and fix them. Humans also ultimately design, build and operate all the malware used for attacks.

There are two other terms that we need to define before we look at the Target breach, our first case study. What happens when a known or suspected cybersecurity breach is detected?

Whenever a known or suspected cybersecurity breach of any significance takes place, a largely manual process known as an ***incident response*** should begin.

***incident response*** *- a prepared set of processes that should be triggered when any known or suspected event takes place that could cause material damage to an organization. The typical stages are (i) verify the event is real and identify the affected areas, (ii) contain the problem (usually by isolating, disabling or disconnecting the affected pieces), (iii) understand and eradicate the root cause, (iv) restore the affected components to their fixed state and (v) review how the process went to identify improvements that should be made. An incident response may also be required to trigger other response* ***procedures****, such as a* ***breach notification procedure****, if any information has been lost that is subject to a notification requirement. For example - the loss of any personal information beyond what might be found in a phone book entry is usually considered a notifiable event.*

***breach notification procedure**** *- some types of information, when suspected or known to be lost or stolen, must, by law, be reported to one or more authorities within a defined time period. The required notification time period varies by regulator, but is often within 24 hours. In addition to reporting the known or suspected loss, the lead organization responsible for the information (referred to as the* ***data*** *owner) is also required to swiftly notify those affected, and later on, to submit a full root cause analysis and information about how they have responded and fixed the issues. To meet these legal obligations, larger companies usually have a pre-defined breach notification procedure to ensure that the timelines are met. The fines for data breaches are usually increased or decreased based on the adequacy of the organization's breach and* ***incident response*** *management.*

As with the rest of this book, the information in the following case studies is based entirely on information openly available in the public domain.

These case studies are intentionally simplified versions of the events. The purpose is to understand the primary events and their causes. We are looking to understand how and why the security gaps were present, rather than analyzing which particular versions of specific software were used at each stage of the attack

.

# 3. Case Study - Target 2013

| | |
|---|---|
| Organization: | **Target** (US Retailer) |
| Breach Dates: | November 27th - December 15th 2013 |
| Date of Discovery: | 15th December 2013 |
| Date of Disclosure: | 18th December 2013 |
| Nature of the Breach: | Loss of customer information including credit card numbers. |
| Scale of the Breach: | 40 to 70 million customer records. |
| Impact: | Estimated to cost Target over $200 million plus brand damage and a resulting decrease in short-term revenues. CEO and CIO both lost their jobs. |

<u>Summary:</u>

A heating, ventilation and air-conditioning (HVAC) sub-contractor had permission to remotely access the Target network for the purpose of remotely monitoring their in-store HVAC systems.

A copy of the supplier's permission credentials was stolen. Analysts believe the thieves used a ***botnet*** (a type of malware) to scrape (steal) these identity and password credentials.

No one immediately detected the theft.

The hackers used the stolen credentials to access the Target network.

They then used network access available through the supplier's credentials to gain access to a part of the network (***network segment***) that contained access to Point of Sale payment systems.

After the breach, darkreading.com revealed that Microsoft had published a case study, available on the Internet, about the Target IT infrastructure, including naming the Microsoft device management software that the company was using. No one knows whether or not the hackers referenced this study to help plan the attack. However, investigators believe that this device management software was used to distribute another type of malware on certain Point of Sale devices that processed card payments.

This malware hid inconspicuously while it recorded and passed credit card data details back out of the Target network using files that were also disguised.

A recently installed FireEye malware detection system in which Target had invested did raise security alerts and notified Target headquarters in late November. For some reason, no immediate action was taken at that time. This is known in security circles as a *failure to trigger an adequate incident response*.

The hackers used hijacked servers outside the Target network to retrieve the stolen data from external drop-off points.

The stolen credit card details appeared for sale on the black market, on specialized websites that exist to sell stolen information.

The US Department of Justice notified Target about the breach on 15th December, and Target initiated immediate corrective steps.

The hackers' access point was closed the same day, and the public was notified on December 18th, once Target was able to assess the impact and confirm that the problem had been addressed.

<u>Root Causes:</u>

There are a number of controls across this chain of events that either failed to be present or to be adequate. Listing those controls is something I can do, but for our purposes we should focus on the primary root causes.

1. Everybody expected and relied upon somebody else's controls to work if their own failed. This is a drawback of poorly implemented 'defense in depth'; you may think that your own security layer or 'piece' is not vital enough to be a point of significant failure. When an alarm was raised, no effective response process was triggered.

2. The security, risk and budget culture was asset and silo focused; nobody adequately considered the big (enterprise) picture of how all those 'little' risks might be stacked together to create a problem of this scale. (See the chapter on 'stacked risks' later in the book.)

3. The security controls and processes that were present were generally set to meet the current minimum security needs and standards. Such standards are generally not updated in a timely manner in response to evolving threats. They generally only protect against issues that have been a concern for a few years. For example, the fact that Target had passed some assessments against the Payment Card Industry Data Security Standards (PCI DSS) did not mean that the security posture was sufficient.

These factors coalesced to create a security posture that contained a large number of potential vulnerabilities.

With credit to Target, they had implemented effective anti-malware. If the alert reports from the anti-malware team had been responded to correctly, that could have prevented the breach.

There were about 50 different security controls that could have been in place to either stop or substantially reduce the duration and scale of this breach. Some of those security control options were not present, and those that were (for example, incident response), failed to operate sufficiently.

It is important to note that each major cyber breach does not occur momentarily. Usually, the breaches that happen today take place over a period of time. This is evidenced by the fact that most breaches are not reported as taking place on a specific date, at a specific time; instead, they are reported to have occurred in a particular month or across a number of months or even years. Target, Home Depot, NSA (Edward Snowden), Sony, Mossack Fonseca, Myspace, Yahoo - you name the breach and look at the duration, and you will consistently find the event involved a span of time.

This is really important to understand correctly. When or if your cybersecurity is breached, in my experience, it will always be true that:

1. Many defense controls (not just one) failed to be in place or to be effective.
2. One or more people miscalculated the risks involved.
3. One or more people either did not respond quickly to an alarm, or had no idea how to trigger the alarm process.

There is also often (but not always) a 4th category:

If the breach happens to be an organization's first, major cyber breach, the senior management team may misguidedly fail to report the event and to quickly engage the right countermeasures. This is a terrible mistake that leads to even greater damage. This fourth mistake did not happen at Target. As soon as Target's senior executives were informed, the incident was managed correctly.

If the incident response had started earlier, when the malware was first detected, analysts believe that the cyber criminals would not have been able to ***exfiltrate*** the information.

**exfiltrate** – *to move something with a degree of secrecy sufficient not to be noticed. Used to describe moving stolen* **data** *unnoticed through detection* **systems***.*

# 4. The Disciplines within Cybersecurity

As groundwork for our next case study, now is a good time to look at the disciplines within cybersecurity.

A popular misconception is that the ability to hack, or break into a computer system, is synonymous with the ability to perform cybersecurity. Although the ability to perform ***ethical hacking*** is a valuable skill, it does not, by itself, equate to an ability to secure an environment.

Criminal hackers only need the ability to find *one* weakness to be successful. On the other hand, effective cybersecurity requires the ability to ensure that *every* significant potential point of weakness is addressed.

Different digital systems require different types and amounts of cybersecurity measures. For a private individual looking to secure his or her own accounts and devices, cybersecurity is relatively straightforward and can include simple steps such as:

- Always maintaining different, complex passwords with over 12 characters for each account of value.
- Keeping one's devices up to date with the latest software patches.
- Installing the most effective anti-malware software.
- Restricting the ability to install software to a separate account. (This then provides a declinable password prompt when most types of unexpected or malicious software tries to install).
- Avoiding surfing to unknown websites or opening unknown links and attachments.
- ...

However, as the scale of the environment that needs protection increases, so does the diversity and scale of the assets. In turn, it takes specialists with diverse skills to protect these diverse assets. The more complex the environment that needs to be protected, the longer the list of skills that are required to help protect it. This is why complex digital environments like those found in large organizations need a range of cybersecurity experts.

If you want to design, build and outfit a large new house and you want to do it well, chances are that you will need to use a group of people with a range of different skills. You are more likely to end up with the best house if you use a blend of the right professionals.

For example, an architect can design a great house, but would offer truly terrible value for any money invested if you put him or her to work on a construction site as a builder.

Similarly, if you let an electrician design your house, the finished product might not end up so well.

Cybersecurity is an even more complex discipline than constructing buildings is. It is also a much newer subject area and is evolving at a much faster rate than any other discipline.

With buildings, at least we have the collective experience of creating them for thousands of years.

But in the world of cybersecurity, being up to date on last year's issues can mean that your knowledge is still out of date. Can you imagine the resulting confusion and growing pains if construction methods changed that fast?

The rate of change in cybersecurity is a real issue in many aspects of life. Years ago, adults were expected to know more about life than children. Today, in many households, when it comes to technology, that relationship is reversed. In many households, a child runs the technology because he or she is better able to understand and keep up with the changes than his or her parents are.

The mind-boggling rate of technological change has even led to new digital technology-related intelligence measurements. General intelligence has long been measured on a scale called the IQ, or Intelligence Quotient. Now there is a measurement called the DQ, or Digital Quotient, being used to measure technology-related intelligence.

You can find tests to measure your DQ online.

A study of digital intelligence in 2014 by Ofcom (the UK communications regulator) found that the average, middle-aged adult scored about 96 on the DQ tests. The average six-year-old scored 98.

They may still be learning right from left, but the average child is likely to know more about technology than the average adult does these days.

This rate of change is partly responsible for driving the need for cybersecurity to be recognized as a dedicated discipline. Since it is a complex subject area undergoing continuous change that requires frequent innovation and modification by practitioners with a blend of different skills, cybersecurity certainly meets the criteria for widely-accepted definitions of what constitutes a discipline - a recognized body of knowledge or a profession in which professionals apply this body of knowledge to their work.

Like other disciplines, cybersecurity cannot be achieved by a single person or a single role. You would not expect to go into a hospital and see just one person who could do everything. Surgeon, hospital administrator, nurse and janitor are very different roles, but all are vital to a fully-functioning hospital. Even within the field of surgery, it is unlikely that a heart surgeon would know much about complex brain surgery.

The same thing is true within cybersecurity.

There are still some organizations that expect to be able to recruit one person to cover all the cybersecurity functions. My advice to cybersecurity professionals is to avoid these positions. Those who try them usually suffer from high levels of stress followed by near-certain failure because of their employers' unrealistic expectations.

With something like construction, it might be possible for one person to achieve a blend of skills over many years that would allow him or her to build a good house.

With cybersecurity, however, the information and necessary skills are changing and are being updated so quickly, it is a challenge to stay on top of the latest information for a single role.

For example, although I have an appreciation of all the roles that can be relevant to cybersecurity and have worked in some of them, my up-to-date knowledge is as a cybersecurity manager. If I went back to performing a different role, I would need to be trained and brought up to date with what to do.

If I had stopped working in a particular cybersecurity role more than 5 years ago, it is likely that my previous knowledge would be so out of date that it might actually be professionally disadvantageous.

So what are the main functions and roles within cybersecurity?

Organizations are still deciding what cybersecurity is and what roles a cybersecurity department should contain. It would be possible to list over 30 different roles in this section, but for clarity, we will look at some of the main functions that should exist either within the cybersecurity team of any major en-enterprise, or accessible to them through a security services company.

In this chapter, cybersecurity **functions** are in bold text. Any roles that can sit within a function are shown in underlined text. There are six main groups of cybersecurity tasks and skills (functions) to consider, with examples of roles underneath:

1) **Management**
   Chief Information Security Officer / Chief Cybersecurity Officer
   Cyber Risk Manager
   Cybersecurity Architect
2) **Cyber Audit & Assessment**
   Audit Manager, Auditor, Assessment Specialist, ...
3) **Event Monitoring and Alerts (Reactive Operations)**
   Security Incident & Events Manager
   Security Incident Responder
   Cybersecurity and Network Intrusion Analysts
4) **Proactive Operations**
   Access Administrators
   Security Device Administrators (***firewalls*** and more)
   Encryption / Cryptography Consultant
   Security Risk Consultants
   Cybersecurity Analysts
5) **Environment Testing**
   Attack & Penetration Testers (Ethical Hackers)
   Vulnerability Assessors
6) **Specialists**
   Security Controls Designer
   External Security Specialist
   Digital Forensics Specialist
   Cryptologist
   Cryptanalyst
   Anti-Malware / Anti-Virus Specialist
   Software Security Specialist

***firewall*** *– is hardware (physical device) or software (computer program) used to monitor and protect inbound and outbound* ***data*** *(electronic information). It achieves this by applying a set of rules. These physical* ***devices*** *or computer pro-*

*grams are usually deployed, at a minimum, at the perimeter of each* ***network*** *access point. Software firewalls can also be deployed on devices to add further security. The rules applied within a firewall are known as the* ***firewall policy.*** *Advanced firewalls are often equipped with other defensive features typical of more* ***unified threat management.***

Collectively, these roles allow for both proactive and reactive security management.

Proactive security is much more beneficial and less expensive than reactive measures are. It is far cheaper to deploy the right security in the first place than it is to fix problems further down the line, especially if any security gaps lead to a substantial loss of information or disruption to customers or business activity.

However, reactive security capabilities have also become a vital component of cybersecurity, as the speed with which any open security issues can be identified and resolved helps to minimize their impact and cost.

Some roles work only on proactive security; some focus on reactive security, and some work on both kinds of cybersecurity measures.

The ways in which these roles fit into either proactive or reactive approaches will be covered in Chapter 6: Basic Cybersecurity Concepts.

## Management

A long-standing question concerning the management function is: What exactly is management supposed to do?

The simple answer is that this function is responsible and accountable for putting the correct **governance** in place.

**governance** – *the methods used by any executive to keep his or her organization on track with the management's goals and within acceptable performance standards. This is usually achieved by establishing* **policies, procedures** *and* **controls** *that match the enterprise's vision, strategy and risk appetite.*

Chief Information Security Officer (CISO) / Chief Cybersecurity Officer

A key principle within any management structure is to have a single point of accountability at the top.

In 2017, there are still too few Chief Cybersecurity Officers or their equivalent, Chief Information Security Officers (CISOs), who occupy a position on the main executive board of each organization. Without this role on the main board, an organization will fail to demonstrate that the main board has the capacity to understand and manage security. Within a few years, it will be unusual for any major organization not to have a CISO or Chief Cybersecurity Officer sitting on the main board.

***Chief Information Security Officer (CISO)*** *– a single point of accountability in any organization for ensuring that an appropriate framework for managing dangers and* ***threats*** *to electronic and physical information* ***assets*** *is operating and effective.*

The Chief Information Security Officer should have an executive strategic focus and ultimate responsibility to ensure the organization has appropriate security processes and resources. Since a digital failure can lead to the termination of an executive board, the CISO must sit on this board and have the full confidence of the Chief Executive and Chief Financial Officers.

The CISO does not make direct business technology decisions, but he or she does manage the processes and reports that help each organization understand and mitigate any security risks. If a Chief Technology Officer (CTO) wants to implement a particular technology, the CISO will not decide if this can happen; instead, the CISO will ensure that the available processes identify the risks and appropriate security measures that should be in place beforehand.

If a new technology has unacceptable risks, the processes set up by the CISO should allow the relevant decision-makers to understand the risks and make their own decision about whether or not to proceed, based on the organizational risk.

A successful CISO has to be a business person first, with excellent political and communication skills, together with a broad understanding of cybersecurity governance (how to manage the ***digital landscape***), a continual eye on emerging technologies and a keen sense of risk and risk management. The CISO also needs to excel in pulling together a strong subordinate security management team.

The CISO must always have final accountability for all security governance items, including ***policies*** and ***procedures***.

***policy*** *– (i) a high-level statement of intent, often a short document, that provides guidance on the principles an organization follows. For example, a basic security policy document could describe the intention for an enterprise to ensure that all locations (physical and electronic) where information for which they are accountable must remain secure from any* ***unauthorized access****. A policy does not usually describe the explicit mechanisms or specific instructions that would be used to achieve or enforce the intentions it expresses; this would be described in a* ***procedure****. (ii) Alternatively, it can also be used to mean the settings (including security settings) inside a* ***software program*** *or operating system.*

***procedure*** *– provides guidance or specific instruction on the process (method) that should be used to achieve an objective. Traditionally provided as a document available to appropriate personnel, but increasingly replaced by instructions that are built into computer* ***systems*** *to enforce the required steps. In a traditional quality model, procedures may reside under a* ***policy*** *as an explicit instruction for meeting a particular policy objective. See also* ***policy*** *definition (i).*

The Chief Information Security Officer defines the security and risk culture for the entire organization, with ultimate accountability for all cybersecurity-related policies and procedures. This role is accountable for ensuring the right control structures are in place to keep risk within acceptable levels, at the same time as these controls provide as much flexibility as possible for the safe use of new and emerging technologies.

A good way to think simply about what a CISO does is to consider that he or she is to technology what the Chief Financial Officer is to the company's money. Each exercises full control and accountability, with external diligence checks taking place occasionally.

There is also a closely related role known as a Chief Information Officer, or CIO. This role is important to security (since information is the new security perimeter); however, the role of the CIO is to look at how to optimize and leverage information value, whereas the role of the CISO is to ensure that those information transactions are governed under secure processes.

Cyber Risk Manager

The CISO somebody needs someone directly under him or her to be responsible for collecting and monitoring the cumulative set of open security **risks** across the digital landscape.

***risk** - a situation involving exposure to significant impact or loss. In formal frameworks, risk can be quantified using probability (often expressed as a percentage) and impact (often expressed as a financial amount). Other parameters for risk can include proximity (how soon a potential risk may be encountered, and information about which **assets**, services, products and processes could be affected).*

The cyber risk manager will usually establish minimum 'materiality' levels (potential probability and impact thresholds) that determine when events and possible threats should be escalated for consideration by more senior management or more knowledgeable specialists.

Effective cyber risk management requires more than just recording information about individual risks. Each risk entry has to capture and explain which digital components and business processes can be impacted; otherwise, the cumulative risk exposure cannot be correlated, analyzed and understood.

It is critical to note that most cybersecurity breaches occur because of cumulative risks. When risks are only looked at individually, without assessing their potential collective impact, it provides a misleading perception of an organization's true level of risk exposure. (See chapter on stacked risks.)

The Cyber Risk Manager not only ensures that appropriate risks are consistently captured but also that the collective risk information picture can be analyzed and understood.

This risk analysis is a critical tool for helping each organization understand which security actions should be assigned the highest priority.

Cybersecurity Architect

Any cybersecurity controls and processes need to be part of a coherent overall plan to be effective; as a well-known saying warns, 'Fail to plan. Plan to fail.' This dictum is originally attributed to the American founding father Benjamin Franklin, but numerous other historic figures, including Winston Churchill, are known for making similar statements.

The importance of designing a strong overall plan is as important in the modern world as it was in Franklin's and Churchill's lifetimes. Although you may be using technology choices from far and wide, unless you want the expense and risk of reinventing the wheel with each choice, you need a security architecture, and that plan requires a cybersecurity architect to construct it.

Rather than spending time designing security features after a technology has been selected, a security architect creates a master plan with standard security components that can be used effectively and quickly each time a new technology needs to be added.

A cybersecurity architect's role is to ensure that there is a clear understanding of the permitted methods for securely integrating and extending an organization's digital ecosystems to interact with others. This includes considering the security of individual mobile applications in any device in which they could exist. It also includes the security standards and requirements expected for remote technologies such as cloud services and critical supplier systems.

For example, using a large number of passwords is really not very secure at all. A security architect can design a framework in which numerous different internal and external technologies can be accessed using exactly the same identity and password, without ever exposing or revealing the password to any other software.

The architect can also design secure, standard options for the flow of information between devices. Whenever a new method of information flow is requested, the security architect should be the one who is involved in reviewing, approving or escalating the issue.

It should be emphasized that especially for large organizations, creating an effective cybersecurity architecture is one of the most (if not *the* most) essential components for running effective cybersecurity.

Without an effective and appropriate cybersecurity architecture model that is available to the Chief Information Officer and to anyone in the organization who is procuring or developing new applications and technologies, there will be a large number of security gaps present. This will create a vicious cycle of costs associated with post-release security incident management and reactive resolution of security gaps that could have been avoided if the specifications had been provided and embedded into the design and release process.

Cybersecurity authorities estimate that the cost of resolving security gaps post-release can be many thousands of times higher than if the correct security controls and architecture had been included initially.

As an example of the value of having embedded specifications, consider a situation in which the acceptable, secure method for users to log into a system is clearly mandated by an organization's cybersecurity architecture. The required login method would be a standard requirement during the construction or procurement of each technology. Exceptions would need to be approved with appropriate justification of the additional risks and costs. Future upgrades to the login technology could happen centrally, easily and inexpensively. Without this specification, the cost to re-visit and repair this ***identity and access management*** component on each active technology can be prohibitively high.

The same thing is true for all of the security standards that should be incorporated by design. If they are adequately integrated into a cybersecurity architecture and provided in an accessible and understandable format to appropriate business owners and procurement departments, the security gaps are less and the future remediation management costs are substantially lower.

## Cyber Audit & Assessment

It is essential to crosscheck the security and integrity of all key technologies, suppliers and processes on a regular basis.

The cyber audit and assurance function exists to check samples of operations to verify whether or not they are being performed securely and correctly - and to identify any significant gaps and any corrective actions that need to be taken.

Audits and assurance are performed based on the key controls that appear in the policies and procedures set by the company management. The policies and procedures are normally aligned to meet any legal requirements or industry standards.

Continuous tracking and reporting on the activities of security administrators can also form part of this function.

Any significant control gaps identified must be tracked through to closure. Any immediate critical risk items must be escalated up to the cyber ***risk register*** (the master list of active risks) or directly to the CISO as appropriate.

## Event Monitoring & Alerts (Reactive Operations)

Digital landscapes are under constant attack. This means that large organizations need technologies and people to continually monitor the real-time information and alerts about attempted intrusions into the network.

### Security Incident and Event Management

It is important to have skilled people ready and able to respond to any cybersecurity problem. Remember what failed to happen when Target's anti-malware program raised an alert? The security incident and event management is the last line of defense function that could have responded in time to save the day.

Large organizations usually have people dedicated to responding to incidents. Smaller organizations often rely on borrowing human resources from other areas whenever an incident occurs. Dedicated resources are much better at incident response because they are more likely to have refined skills, knowledge and tools to rapidly perform the root cause analysis and corrective measures required. Dedicated resources are also more likely to be available to respond quickly.

Usually, there will be a Security Incident Responder on call at all times to ensure an immediate response to any event such as a ***denial of service*** (DoS) or malware attack.

> ***Denial of Service (DoS)*** *- an* ***attack*** *designed to stop or disrupt peoples' use of organizations' systems. Usually, a particular section of an enterprise is targeted; for example, a specific* ***network, system, digital device*** *type or function. These attacks usually originate from, and are targeted at, devices accessible through the Internet. If the attack is from multiple source locations, it is referred to as a* ***Distributed Denial of Service, or DDoS*** *attack.*

### Cybersecurity & Network Intrusion Analysts

This role is responsible for measuring, monitoring and managing the operational status of all assets and information flows that are directly under the control or accountability of the organization. This includes all software, hardware, network devices, communication channels and third party (external) landscape items that can be a potential source of vulnerabilities.

This is usually coordinated through a combination of device and network monitoring software, together with other investigative tools. These pieces of information are usually collected to form status dashboards and automated alerts that operate around the clock.

Larger organizations will usually have a security operations center (SOC), which essentially contains one or more offices where real-time threats are monitored and managed.

The specifications for the level of control are set by the policies, procedures and baseline standards put in place by the cybersecurity management team, including the CISO and cybersecurity architect.

Any day-to-day operational gaps or deficiencies are also resolved (tracked to resolution) by this security operations team. Any significant gaps or deficiencies in policies and procedures are reported to the cyber assurance function, along with recommendations to initiate improvements.

These analysts also perform security monitoring, including the analysis of logs to help detect and report incidents.

Any major incident detected by the network intrusion analysts must immediately trigger the incident response procedure.

The analysts from this team are usually also part of the incident response team, under the direction of the Security Incident and Event Management function. They are usually best placed to help assess damage and impact should any incidents take place.

Members of this team are also valuable consulting assets for the creation of new security solutions and the hardening of existing security standards.

## Proactive Operations

In addition to the security incident and security monitoring personnel who help detect and respond to known or suspected incidents, there are also many other roles that may help to sustain an effective and secure digital landscape.

This is a brief and very basic list of some of the primary roles that are involved in the day-to-day proactive management of security.

Access Administrators

This role performs the actions that set up and manage access to devices and systems that are used to run each organization.

Most organizations monitor these administrators closely and prohibit them from any operational use of the system other than that which is necessary to their job of adding or removing other peoples' access.

For example, if a person administers the access rights to a financial system, it would be important to prohibit that same administrator from performing any operational transactions, such as raising or approving a purchase order.

Access administration roles should be rotated (changed) periodically, and any access changes that are implemented on highly sensitive systems should require at least 2 access administrators to process (a proposer and an approver).

It is usual for access administration roles to have their activities recorded in electronic audit trails and for any suspicious activity patterns to automatically raise alerts. For example, if an access permission is granted and then removed on the same day, this is known to be an indicator of potential fraud.

Security Device Administrators

There is a wide and growing range of security technologies that are used to run any medium or large organization.

The people who perform any configuration or management of the technologies that are used to detect, block or allow digital traffic are in a privileged position that is a prime target for any cyber attack. For this reason, people who manage firewalls, network devices and security-specific technologies such as ***data loss prevention*** software are considered to have privileged access that benefits from processes that supervise their privileged access.

**Data Loss Prevention (DLP)** – *this term can describe both (i) the technologies and (ii) the strategies used to help stop information from being taken out of an organization without the appropriate authorization. Software technologies can use heuristics (patterns that fit within certain rules) to recognize, alert and/or block* **data** *extraction activities on* **digital devices**. *For example, a DLP technology may prohibit specific types of file attachments from being sent out via Internet mail services. These technologies can also prevent or monitor many other attempts at removing or copying data. There are workarounds that can be used by skilled*

> ***hackers*** *to evade detection by these solutions, including* ***encryption*** *and fragmentation. Although these solutions are becoming an essential line of defense, the most secure environments aim to prevent any significant set of data from being available for export in the first place. For this reason, Data Loss Prevention is often thought of as the last line of defense (a final safety net if all other security controls have not been successful).*

Standard good cybersecurity practices incorporate processes and technologies that provide effective oversight of these roles. These measures usually make use of a ***privileged account management*** system (PAMS).

> ***privileged account management*** *– the* ***systems****, technologies and processes used to monitor and control the activities of* ***privileged accounts****.*

Many of the technologies operated by security administrators have the capability, if misused or accessed by any hostile party, to cause massive business disruptions. Some security technologies have the ability to prevent the entire environment(s) they are protecting from working.

The roles that configure and maintain the digital gateways, security, databases and communication channels are therefore usually subject to close monitoring, audit trails that trace their actions, secondary approval and automated software that raises alerts or blocks any suspicious or unauthorized actions.

Encryption / Cryptography Specialist

This role acts as an advisor or administrator of safe key management processes and also advises on appropriate encryption / cryptography standards.

With the increase in the amount of information that is now encrypted (ciphered from plain text into secret formats), large organizations now have to design and operate something called a cryptographic key architecture. This architecture allows them to ensure that the keys used to encrypt and decrypt information are readily available when and where they are needed.

Cryptographic key architecture is part of the security architecture, designed with input from cryptography specialists.

Security Risk Consultant

Whenever a new type of technology, device or communication channel is being considered, it is advisable to assess the risk before deciding whether or not to implement it.

This could be the risk from a new technology, a new supplier, a new cloud service or any other 'new' activity that will result in information of any value being transacted.

The security risk consultant advises on the security risk process design and provides consultative assistance to the business each time a risk assessment process is run. This will be discussed further in later chapters.

## Environment Testing

One of the areas of cybersecurity that most people get excited about is **ethical hacking** and **red team** processes.

> ***ethical hacking*** *– the process by which supportive* ***(white-hat)*** *penetration testing experts assist in finding security weaknesses and* ***vulnerabilities.***
>
> ***red team*** *– when testing for potential* ***exploits*** *affecting any critical or sensitive* ***system,*** *infrastructure or website, a team of* ***penetration testers*** *is usually used. This term (red team) is used to describe the group of penetration testers working together on this type of objective.*

'Red teaming' is an exercise that seeks to verify if and how any gaps in the security of an environment could be compromised. In the exercise, the red team is resourced with ethical hackers and a blue team (defensive group) of security personnel seeks to identify and block their attempts.

Although this is one method of testing the cybersecurity of an environment, it has several drawbacks.

- It is very expensive to do.
- Unless conducted before an environment is live, it is reactively uncovering issues at a time when it will be potentially far more expensive to fix.
- It requires the permission of the owner of an environment, which often excludes the environments of greatest risk (such as supplier systems).

Although red team exercises are a lot of fun, they tend to make up a fraction of a percent of any cybersecurity budget expenditures.

However, there is a very valuable version that is more consistently used and is more proactive in nature: ***penetration tests***.

Penetration Testers (also sometimes referred to as ***ethical hackers***)

***Penetration testers*** perform checks and scans for potential exploits across any new system or website before it is operational and on a periodic (repeating) basis defined by the organization's procedures and security posture. Any exploits (vulnerabilities) discovered are usually assigned a criticality level and resolved if their criticality level is higher than the organization's acceptable standard.

**ethical hacker** – *an alternative name for a* **penetration tester.**

**penetration test** *(also known as an attack and penetration test or pen. test) – checks and scans on any application, system or website to identify any potential security gaps (***vulnerabilities***) that could be exploited. Once the vulnerabilities are identified, this process then goes on to identify the extent to which these vulnerabilities could be leveraged in an attack (the penetration possibilities). Usually these checks are performed in a test area and emulate the same techniques that could be used by an attacker. This is to prevent any inadvertent operational disruption. The checks are typically conducted before any application or site is first used, and also on a periodic (repeating) basis; for example, each time the program is updated or every 6 months. Any significant gaps must be addressed (fixed) in a timeframe appropriate to the scale of the risk. Not to be confused with the term vulnerability assessment, which only identifies gaps without examining how they could be leveraged. See also* **pivoting.**

**penetration tester** – *a person who performs simulated attempts at* **attack** *on a target system or application on behalf of the organization that owns or controls it. See also* **penetration test** *and* **pivoting.**

Penetration tests are almost always performed on a copy of a live system and not on the live system itself. This is to prevent any inadvertent operational disruption.

Penetration testing is considered to be an essential ingredient for the realization and release of any software or system that has security by design. It helps by verifying whether all of the expected security has been achieved.

Vulnerability Assessors

A process called ***vulnerability assessment*** is typically run using specialized software.

> **vulnerability assessment** – *the identification and classification of security gaps in a computer, software* ***application, network*** *or other section of a* ***digital landscape.*** *This is usually a passive identification technique that aims only to identify the gaps, without exploring how those gaps could be used in an attack. This should not be confused with a* ***penetration test****, which may include information from a vulnerability assessment, but which will go on to explore how any vulnerabilities can be exploited.*

These checks are usually performed on live and operational environments and are intentionally passive (non-aggressive) to prevent inadvertent operational disruption.

The vulnerability assessor manages the vulnerability assessments and the management of the results produced by the process. These assessments can be conducted periodically but are increasingly being performed continuously in real time.

## Other Roles

This is not a full and exhaustive list. These additional roles are just examples of other, more specialized roles that can also be important to a cybersecurity team, depending on its size and purpose.

Security Controls Designer

This person can support the cybersecurity area by analyzing the exact requirements (purpose and intention) for any new security control and by proposing the most efficient, effective and least-disruptive design.

External Security Specialists

These specialists can be very useful in helping to advise, augment or educate the internal cybersecurity team on any matters or subject areas that are unfamiliar to them or for which they have an insufficient time allocation. External specialists can also be useful for temporary or part-time roles. The main criterion for selecting these adjunct team members is to first verify that they do actually have the missing skills the team needs.

Digital Forensics

Following any legal issue that arises from a cybersecurity incident, a digital forensics specialist preserves, rebuilds and recovers electronic information. This role is usually a key part of any law enforcement or legal action involving the misuse of digital devices.

Anti-Malware / Anti-Virus Specialists

These specialists help to analyze, counteract, report and defend against new types of malicious software. They are particularly useful during ***zero-day*** attacks.

***zero-day*** *– refers to the very first time a new type of* ***exploit*** *or new piece of* ***malware*** *is discovered. At that point in time, none of the* ***anti-virus, anti-malware*** *or other defenses may be set up to defend against the new form of exploit.*

Software Security Specialist

This specialist ensures that software is 'secure by design' by incorporating security features into both the construction process and the features specifications. Other duties may include running automated and manual scans through the program itself (known as the source code) to guard against any ***backdoor*** or other unfriendly insertions by programmers.

***backdoor*** *– a covert method of accessing software or a device that bypasses the normal authentication requirements.*

Cryptologist

A cryptologist, or encryption code-maker, performs research to create stronger encryption algorithms. This is usually a role reserved for security software companies and the cybersecurity functions within nation states' government agencies.

Cryptanalyst

This role analyzes encrypted information to decrypt and reveal the information. Essentially, this person is an encryption code-breaker. His or her skills can be especially useful in anti-malware companies because any new malware itself is usually encrypted.

These were only basic descriptions of the main functions and roles that may be required within the cybersecurity team of any major enterprise.

Keep in mind that people are sometimes required to cover a number of these roles and that a job title often has little to do with the actual tasks and duties involved.

Two areas only partially covered above but becoming increasingly important are:

- Putting together threat intelligence teams across these disciplines that are tasked with predicting and pre-empting the most likely threats and exploits to emerge.
- Ensuring that the correct contingency and restoration plans are ready to go, in the event that a disaster (technical or natural) takes place.

Contingency plans are usually known as ***Business Continuity Plans***.

***Business Continuity Plan*** *– (abbreviation BCP) an operational document that describes how an organization can restore its critical products or services to its customers, should a substantial event that causes disruption to normal operations occur.*

Business continuity plans are an entire subject area and discipline in their own right. A single organization often has multiple business continuity plans to ensure that each location, product and service can be individually restored.

Since technologies are often used across multiple sites, products and services, the actual plans for restoring a digital system are only referenced by a business continuity plan and not contained within it.

The restoration plan for a digital or electronic system is known as either a ***Technical Disaster Recovery Plan*** or simply as a ***Disaster Recovery Plan***.

***Technical Disaster Recovery Plan*** *– an operational document that describes the exact process, people, information and* ***assets*** *required to put any electronic or digital system back in place within a timeline defined by the* ***business continuity***

*plan. If there are multiple business continuity plans that reference the same Technical Disaster Recovery Plan, the restoration time used must meet the shortest time specified in any of the documents.*

Although these disciplines (business continuity and disaster recovery) already exist separately in any major organization, they are an example of additional roles that exist in organizations in which cybersecurity must be represented, considered and embedded.

You might not think that natural disasters relate to technical resilience, but think of the tsunami-induced disaster at Fukushima, and think how a hacker thinks. If you want to take out a digital system, brute force can often be more effective than technical prowess. It is essential to think about all the little things, but it's also important not to forget the other events that can potentially wipe out your technological inventory.

There are many things to consider when putting together an effective cybersecurity team that is capable of addressing all the technical, environmental, and human factors that contribute to cybersecurity resilience and incidents. I think a statement made by the Head of Cybersecurity for the Department of Homeland Security offers sound advice on this subject:

If you want a strong team that can help you stay ahead of cybersecurity issues, it is wise to make sure your team is EGGE. That means that if you are looking for a strong team to run an enterprise's cybersecurity, you should put together a set of people that are:

- Ethnically diverse
- Geographically diverse
- Gender diverse
- Educationally diverse

These are very wise words indeed. You cannot hope to identify the potential weaknesses your opposition might find if you have a group of people who have a smaller inventory of knowledge.

# 5. Case Study - Edward Snowden 2013

| | |
|---|---|
| Organization(s): | Hawaii NSA Regional Operations Center |
| Breach Dates: | Unknown (March 2013?) to June 2013 |
| Date of Discovery: | June 2013 |
| Date of Disclosure: | June 2013 |
| Nature of the Breach: | Australian, British and American classified documents stolen and publicly revealed. |
| Scale of the Breach: | 250,000 to 2 million documents. |
| Impact: | Political instability and trade relations damage. Direct personal danger to service personnel named in some documents. |

Summary:

There is plenty written on the subject of Edward Snowden. Here we will only focus on the facts that help us to understand what happened to allow such a huge cybersecurity breach.

There are 3 potential sources of information about what happened:

- Information from the US National Security Agency and US Government
- Edward Snowden himself
- Speculators

We need to stay based in fact, so we will focus on reports from the first 2 sources that present consistent information and will leave speculation out of the equation.

Edward Snowden joined a company called Booz Allen in March 2013. Booz Allen was one of several companies that performed contract work for the US National Security Agency.

The US government requires extensive pre-screening for companies and people who have access to any system or systems that can access sensitive government information, so Snowden himself was subject to strict pre-hire assessments.

Snowden's pre-employment screening assessments reportedly indicated that he was reasonably reliable and that it was safe to hire him for the Booz Allen role:

- He had already worked with privileged access to government systems for many years without any issues.
    - Snowden worked directly for the US Central Intelligence Agency between 2006 and 2009, where he proved to be extremely good at computer network security.
    - He then joined Dell, working on NSA contracts, and allegedly went on to advise US government agencies on strategies to protect their networks from attack.
- His family had a strong history of government and military service.

Snowden himself had not previously demonstrated any behavior that triggered any reported concerns about his ethics, personality or outlook. At least, if there were ever any signs, they had not resulted in a revocation of his previous security status and were not available to Booz Allen.

He had accepted a pay decrease when he joined Booz Allen.

Whatever the reasons were that Snowden provided to Booz Allen for accepting a lesser salary, they were plausible enough to pass through the screening processes.

Snowden himself identified 3 key events that changed his outlook.

1) The personal discomfort he felt when he discovered the amount of personal data the US and UK governments were collecting and reviewing about their own private citizens.
2) The absence of sufficient governance mechanisms to secure the environments and report any misuse of information at all government levels.
3) In March 2013, he described reaching a breaking point when he watched a top US official in the security service 'directly lie to Congress under oath.'

The precise tasks and duties for which Edward Snowden was responsible are unclear and vary in different accounts. It is unlikely that he had the range of access and responsibility he himself sometimes describes. All parties do, however, confirm that he did have certain security administration privileges and that security administration was his primary role.

A further certainty is that Edward Snowden knew his subject area (network security) extremely well.

With years of insider knowledge, together with a small amount of privileged access and a disaffected outlook, he had a combination of motive, capability and opportunity to internally exploit the organization's cybersecurity vulnerabilities.

To safeguard operations, it is a usual control to monitor system administrators closely and to prohibit them from also having operational access to the information in the same system. For example, if you administered peoples' access to their bank accounts, it would be a normal control for you to be prohibited from ever having or granting yourself permission to access those same accounts and the information they contain.

Most high-security systems contain audit trails that record, trace, prevent and alert suspicious access. However, recording who has ever accessed specific pieces of intelligence or other sensitive information is a double-edged sword. Even top officials may need to occasionally access something without leaving a record of that access.

In Snowden's case, there were some audit trails and logs in place designed to monitor for suspicious actions, but he was either able to bypass them or to ensure that they did not raise any immediate, significant alerts.

Most high-security environments also monitor anybody with privileged access very closely. Edward Snowden had a level of access privilege low enough to allow him to work independently but high enough to misuse to get into other higher value agency systems and devices. This is evident from the extremely large number of files he was able to extract without being noticed.

After extracting the files, he used several ***USB*** thumb drives to take them out of his workplace. He apparently had no problem carrying these drives in and out of the facility.

***USB*** *– acronym for* ***U****niversal* ***S****erial* ***B****us. This is a standard connector that exists on most computers, smartphones, tablets and other physical electronic* ***devices*** *that allow other electronic devices to be connected. Used for attaching a range of devices including keyboards, mice, external displays, printers and external storage devices.*

The exact amount of information that Edward Snowden stole remains unknown. Estimates by the US government and by Snowden himself range from around 250,000 to 1.7 million documents.

Root Cause Analysis:

There is no single root cause responsible for this breach. It is again true that a number of standard security controls were not in place, and these lapses provided Snowden with the opportunity to perpetrate the theft.

Reviewing the available information, the primary causes were:

- There was **insufficient monitoring and evaluation of administrator activities.**

  US government departments began to stipulate 'mandatory vacations' for security administrators after the event. This is an indication that the rogue activities would likely have been discovered even if Snowden had been rotated out of his role for a few days.
- **Toxic accumulation of domain knowledge.**

  The amount of domain-specific, accumulated security knowledge that Snowden obtained was too high for any individual to have. This meant that he knew exactly how and where he could gain access to sensitive files without fear of immediate detection. His knowledge of security was not the issue; instead, the fact that he was able to gather enough insider knowledge to pinpoint specific and significant security gaps was the shortcoming that led to the breach. As with all 'secret' information, various aspects of security knowledge need to be broken into pieces and never made available to the same person.
- **Toxic accumulation of privileges.**

  This is a term often used by banks. As someone moves through different jobs in an organization, his or her prior permissions are often accidentally left in place. Over a period of years, this may allow the person to operate across multiple systems in ways that each department would never have considered.
- **The rules on only assigning 'Least Privilege' were not applied.**

  When anyone is given access permission to anything, it should be on the basis of the minimum rights they require to do what they need to do. For some roles, especially administrators and programmers, it can be tempting but inadvisable to provide full access, as this diminishes security administration overheads but increases security vulnerabilities.

- **Incorrect or inadequate classification of some assets and information.**

  Some organizations keep a detailed map of their complete network or a comprehensive security plan, complete with information about every layer of security present. These records can serve as building blueprints for identifying the weakest and most vulnerable points of entry, but they are also often subject to much less security than the information they protect. For instance, the security plan might reveal that there is a network device that is the gateway to the organization's most classified and confidential information. I personally have been given security and network plans like this during an external audit. Although these documents are designed to evidence a strong security posture, granting access to this document, or even having it all in one place, is evidence to the contrary.

- **Inadequate system and process auditing.**

  Just like in the Target case, a number of security controls were missing. This time, part of the reason (as stated by Edward Snowden) was that nobody regularly and accurately checked (audited) to ascertain whether or not the right controls were in place. Snowden was not the only person who knew this, and many others with insider knowledge made similar comments after the incident occurred. Secret environments are often, intentionally unaccountable. In this case, the degree of unaccountability allowed it to escape audit, which in turn made it possible for a substantial number of security gaps to persist.

- **Certain functions that involve privileged access should require 2 people to operate.**

  This did not happen in this case.

- **Physical security was complacent and based on trust.**

  Employees and contractors knew that it was unlikely that they would be searched for devices like small USB storage devices. It is likely that there were no random searches and that 'known' people came and went as they liked.

It is clear that since this event occurred, the National Security Agency believes they need to focus on improving their pre-screening processes. However, it is doubtful that more robust pre-screening alone would have detected any security issues.

Snowden had a track record of years of reliable service and much experience passing pre-screening checks. It is wishful thinking to believe that more stringent screening would have been an easy way to prevent the breach. In Edward Snowden's case, the only potential indicator of a hidden motive was his willingness to accept a drop in pay.

Improved screening for employees and contractors with potentially subversive motives is still a good idea. There is a lot of ongoing work on how personality profiling can help with this process. This research is being conducted for a very valid reason - people are always the weakest link in the cybersecurity defense chain. For that reason, we dedicate an entire chapter to human factors later in the book.

We should also remember that Edward Snowden did not work for the NSA. He worked for a contractor. Contractors and other suppliers usually do exactly what the customer asks for, and if they are clever, they do nothing extra. Doing extra things for free erodes margins. What does this mean? It means that any third party will not be giving away free security enhancements - they will only (usually) do exactly what you asked for and paid for.

That is not to say that Booz Allen did anything wrong. It is just a general comment about the fact that any commercially astute supplier will only do what it is specifically paid to do and no more.

In my own years of auditing suppliers, I have found that they are often very good at highlighting and recommending fixes for security gaps. However, since closing those gaps normally has a price attached, the customer often makes the decision to live with the gaps.

Edward Snowden was an insider who gained a toxic combination of too much inside knowledge, too much unsupervised privilege, dissatisfaction with his own life path and intense dissatisfaction with some of the actions of a few powerful people.

He knew more about the security vulnerabilities than the people trying to keep it secure did. The bottom line was that there were a lot of open security vulnerabilities in place.

So was Edward Snowden a whistleblower or a traitor? That is not for us to determine. It is, however, relevant to look at a few additional facts.

Edward Snowden did alert the public to the degree and tactics that some governments were using to monitor peoples' digital systems. He also identified the presence of authorized backdoors that many of the major social media technologies had provided for use by government agencies. These agencies find the backdoors useful, as they bypass the need to put large amounts of resources into breaking the **encryption** layer.

**encryption** - *the act of encoding messages so that if they are intercepted by an unauthorized party, they cannot be read unless the encoding mechanism can be deciphered.*

Conversely, any cybersecurity expert knows that backdoors are a bad idea because the vulnerabilities they create are useful to attackers and usually far outweigh the benefits. For example, imagine what would happen if a bank had 16 security layers on the main entrance for customers and a single unguarded door at the back for staff. Which entry point would you attack?

Based on these revelations, it can be argued that Edward Snowden's activities did serve the public interest to some degree. However, most whistleblowers carefully select evidence to reveal a problem, rather than blindly releasing hundreds of thousands to millions of sensitive documents like Snowden did.

According to Edward Snowden's own admissions, he released thousands of classified government documents to journalists even though he had never reviewed the documents himself

# 6. Basic Cybersecurity Concepts

So far, we have defined what cybersecurity is, where it came from, how it can go wrong and what kinds of roles are involved in putting together an effective cybersecurity team.

In this section, we look at some of the basic building blocks of cybersecurity.

When I wrote the first edition if this book, there were no solid cybersecurity frameworks. Since then, both NIST (the US National Institute for Standards & Technology) and ISACA have produced very good reference models.

Recent cybersecurity frameworks tend to break the steps involved in building an effective cybersecurity system into five or more stages:

- Identify (your valuable assets)
- Protect (with appropriate security)
- Detect (any compromised account or device)
- Respond (quarantine the problem and identify countermeasures)
- Recover (replace, restore or otherwise fix compromised assets)

This chapter is mainly devoted to looking at the first two of the stages and discussing what they involve.

| | | |
|---|---|---|
| Proactive | √ Identify<br>√ Protect | This chapter – the importance of security by design. |
| Reactive | √ Detect<br>√ Respond<br>√ Recover | Chapter 14 – 'What to do when things go wrong,' |

It is the proactive stages (identify and protect) where security can be applied with the greatest impact and efficiency.

Although it is essential to have reactive capabilities too, it costs thousands of times more to correct a security issue or problem than it does to include appropriate security measures in the first place.

As an example, in February 2017, a small error in the code for a major Internet service provided by Cloudflare was discovered. The error had slipped through testing and into release some months earlier. This 'minor bug' (later named 'cloudbleed'), once identified, was easily fixed within minutes. However, the consequences of the bug required corrective efforts from hundreds of thousands of people, who had to delete and reset information that might have been accidentally exposed by it.

However, organizations face the additional challenge that it has become untenable to maintain a perfect level of proactive cybersecurity throughout their digital systems.

This means that in addition to proactively identifying and protecting their information (the first two steps of identify and protect), they also need to have effective ways to detect any intrusions or disruptions as early as possible and to then address and fix the problems.

In this chapter, we will look at the following concepts that are critical foundations to identify, protect, detect, and recover information, systems and devices:

- Information Classification
  - Confidentiality, Integrity, Availability & Consent
- Cybersecurity Defense Points
  - Data, Devices, Applications, Systems and Networks
- Cybersecurity Control Types
  - Physical, Procedural, Legal & Technical
- Cybersecurity Control Modes:
  - Preventive, Detective & Corrective

Classification, controls, and related concepts are indeed all relevant in fulfilling the primary objectives of any type of cybersecurity.

I have heard it said that Cybersecurity is about only one thing: **Money**.

This is untrue. Cybersecurity is about **power**. It might be political power, it could be financial power; it is often a combination of the two.

For example, when the CENTCOM (US Central Command) Twitter account was compromised for 40 minutes by the Islamic State in January 2015, the motive was not monetary; it was political. The objective was to create discomfort and a sense of insecurity by openly demonstrating a security gap and sending out political messages through it.

If I have good cybersecurity, I control my own power. If I have cybersecurity gaps that allow access to anything significant, someone else can use my digital devices for their own financial or political gain at my expense.

The fact is that we do not necessarily have to have great cybersecurity everywhere. We do need great cybersecurity on items that can directly or indirectly cause us financial or political damage.

So how do we determine what is significant?

To simplify cybersecurity we need to go right back to basics. What is cybersecurity?

Cybersecurity, in its simplest form, is intended to protect digital devices from being exploited or compromised.

Whenever an experienced cybersecurity manager looks at the cybersecurity position of anything, we ask ourselves this question:

***Do I feel confident that we have sufficiently considered and addressed all of the possible methods that might be used to attack or compromise this digital device or digital landscape?***

To become even slightly comfortable with being able to respond to that, we need to consider (i) all locations within our digital landscape and (ii) all the potential vectors (methods) that could be a point of failure or attack and (iii) most importantly - *the inherent value that each digital location has*.

The higher the impact and value of any part of the digital landscape, the greater the pain the organization will suffer if it is compromised. That means the most valuable digital locations need the greatest levels of cyber protection.

This is exactly what we ourselves do in our everyday lives. We make sure that we put the greatest amount of security on our most valuable items. Money, car, jewelry; all of these are usually protected with security proportionate to their value. If you have $1 you are probably okay to have it in your pocket. If you have one million dollars, you probably will not want to carry it around.

Similarly, if you have a beaten up wreck of a car, you will probably not worry about parking it anywhere, but if you have a car with a million dollar price tag, you will probably be more careful.

All we are doing in cybersecurity is applying these same principles to electronic devices and services that use and manage data. If these devices and services use and manage data worth millions, we need to take more precautions than if they only handle a single dollar's worth of data.

We call these precautions ***controls***.

> ***control** - (in the context of security and compliance) a method of regulating something, often a process, technology or behavior, to achieve a desired outcome, usually resulting in the reduction of **risk**. Depending on how it is designed and used, any single control may be referred to as preventive, detective or corrective.*

We first need to **identify** what to protect:

- We have to sort out which groups of information are most valuable in order to understand their comparative security requirements and priority. This is called ***information classification***.
- Once we know what information we are defending, we can determine where it is located and where it passes through. These will become our ***cyber defense points***.

We can then work out how to **protect** those assets appropriate to the potential value and impact they could have:

- At each of these defense points, we can use a range of physical, procedural, technical and legal security controls. These are our ***control types***.
- Some cyber defenses are proactive, some are detective (reactive) and some are corrective. These are our cybersecurity ***control modes***.

We will now expand and explain each of those steps in order.

## Identify

Before we can protect anything effectively and efficiently, we need to understand what we have and just what potential value it has.

Remember the analogy that just like water flows through plumbing, information flows through technologies. If you have little idea about which information of value you have or where it is flowing, you also have little to no chance of applying appropriate security to protect it.

It is not practical to apply high levels of security to everything. It is also inadvisable to leave high-value information in areas without high levels of security. To be able to apply the correct level of security, it is essential to understand that the value of different types of information determines how much protection it requires.

There are parts of each digital landscape with very low value information that could be made public with no damage, and other parts that transact and store information so sensitive that we need to take quite extreme security measures. Getting cybersecurity right requires a comprehensive approach, especially as low value, low security areas are often used as routes into the higher value areas.

Now that any digital landscape can go far beyond a network perimeter - for example, into mobile devices, cloud services and supplier systems - it is not sufficient or effective to simply inventory and protect the assets inside an organization's network.

So how do we perform the identification process?

Fortunately, the clue is in job titles like Chief *Information* Security Officer.

Everything we need to protect has one thing in common; **it has information of value flowing through it.** If we identify all the sets of information we want to protect, that will lead us to an understanding of all the digital devices, applications and services that it runs through, even if they are not within our network.

To achieve this in any organization, we use two processes: (1) The creation or collation of an information asset register (a list of the sets of data we need to evaluate and protect) and (2) the evaluation of each information asset to help us understand how we should be protecting it. The second process is part of a task known as information classification.

## Information Classification

Each group of information is not of equal value.

If we want to get our cybersecurity posture correct, we need to create categories that help us to differentiate the value and danger inherent in each major set of information we have.

The process of determining the value, impact and sensitivity of data is known as ***information classification***.

***information classification**** – *the assignment of one or more values to a collection of knowledge that help us understand how alike it is to any other set of knowledge. For information security, this is usually achieved by assigning values against* ***confidentiality, integrity*** *and* ***availability,*** *or CIA. A fourth category,* ***consent,*** *is also sometimes used when the set of knowledge includes information on private individuals. This assignment of categories can then be used to more easily select the security and recovery approach appropriate to the information's value and impact.*

***confidentiality*** – *the assignment of a value to a set of information to indicate the level of secrecy and the access restrictions required to prevent unauthorized people from viewing it. A typical example of a confidentiality scale is: (i) Public Use (ii) Internal Use (iii) Confidential (iv) Strictly Confidential and (v) Restricted.*

***integrity**** – *a value that can be assigned to a set of information to indicate how sensitive it is to degradation of accuracy (such as unauthorized modification) or* ***data*** *loss. Loss in this context is about losing information without the ability for anyone to recover it from the system it was entered into (it is not about theft). This value is often expressed or translated into a scale of time. The integrity value assigned to any system or application is used to set the frequency that the information is subject to backup, or in very sensitive systems with no data loss permitted, establishes the need for a permanent secondary failover system.*

***availability**** – *the assignment of a value to a set of information to indicate how much disruption or outage the owner considers to be acceptable. This is often expressed or translated into a scale of time.* ***Data*** *with the highest possible availability rating would be required to be readily accessible at all times (no downtime permitted), often through the use of a fully redundant failsafe.*

***consent*** – *when personal electronic information is involved, there are often legal constraints that govern how the* ***data*** *can be used and where the information can be viewed, stored, transmitted or otherwise processed. In these circumstances, permission is often required from each individual to specify which information can be collected, where it can be processed and for how long it will be retained. These permissions can be represented by a series of tags on individual records or on the full data set. The attributes that require explicit permission may include, but are not limited to, country of origin, permission for export, limitations of use, retention and notification requirements.*

Information classification is not a new practice. It has been an established part of information security for many decades.

It is also the most fundamental cornerstone for effective cybersecurity.

Without information classification, you have no idea whether you are protecting something of high value or low value.

This is also sometimes referred to as data classification. The only difference between data classification and information classification is that 'data' only refers to electronic information, whereas 'information' can also include physical forms such as paper records.

As each information asset is categorized, it enables follow-on processes to be run to identify the digital devices, applications, communication channels and other dependencies. This in turn allows the organization to understand what needs to be protected and how robust the protection needs to be.

This process can also identify locations where information is flowing that you don't want it to go. By controlling where information of value is permitted to flow, we can then reduce the amount of effort required to protect it.

Cyber Defense Points.

Once you know what the most valuable information assets are, you also need to know where they are located before you can formulate an effective cyber defense.

At this point, we are still only identifying what needs to be protected.

Classifying our information lets us know *what* to defend, but we still need to understand *where* to defend it. The **cyber defense points** are the digital locations *where* we could add cybersecurity controls.

Only by understanding what a cyber defense point contains and transacts can I ensure that the security controls on it are proportionate to its value and the risks to which it is exposed.

There are 6 layers of digital defense points that are typically considered for cybersecurity:

*i)* **Data** – *any information in electronic or digital format.*

ii) **Devices** - *any hardware used to create, modify, process, store or transmit data. Computers, smartphones and USB drives are all examples of devices.*

iii) **Applications** - *any programs (software) that reside on any device. Usually, programs exist to create, modify, process, store, inspect or transmit specific types of data.*

iv) **Systems** - *groups of applications that operate together to serve a more complex purpose.*

v) **Networks** - *the group name for a collection of devices, wiring and applications used to connect, carry, broadcast, monitor or safeguard data. Networks can be physical (use material assets such as wiring) or virtual (use applications to create associations and connections between devices or applications.)*

vi) *Other* **communication channels** - *any other routes used to transmit or transfer any electronic data of value between devices*

You may be wondering why 'data' itself is considered to be a cyber defense point. The reason is simple; there are security controls that can be applied directly to data. For example, data can be encoded (encrypted) so that even if it is intercepted or copied, it does not become accessible without further effort.

The importance of any item is determined by what it does rather than what it is.

We might have 2 physically identical computers. However, if one of these computers is empty and the other contains pre-stock market announcements about a company's financial information, the security requirements will be different.

The differentiating factor is determined by the value, impact and therefore the sensitivity of the contents.

If we start by identifying the most sensitive data (the electronic information with the highest value and impact if compromised or lost), we can then understand which cyber defense points it exists in and flows through.

This approach will help us identify and prioritize where and how to put appropriate security on our digital landscape in a logical order.

This is also where the skills of a security architect can be very useful. Instead of accepting our landscape as it is, a security architect can help by evaluating our needs and creating a simpler and easier-to-defend digital landscape with a smaller and less-varied set of cyber defense points.

A security architecture approach provides the opportunity to re-design the components through which our information flows to make the cyber defense points easier and more cost-effective to defend.

# Protect

Cybersecurity Control Types

We know what to defend (using information classification) and where to defend it (cyber defense points). We still need to know how to defend it.

There are 4 major categories of security controls that can be used when constructing cybersecurity protection:

a. Physical
b. Technical
c. Procedural
d. Legal (also referred to as regulatory or compliance controls)

If I want to keep some gold bullion safe, I can place it in a locked, alarmed and isolated vault that would make it extremely difficult to steal.

If I have a digital memory card, packed with sensitive information but not attached to anything else, I have exactly the same possibilities.

At this point, although my data is electronic, it is in a physical form.

Potentially, this memory card is more secure than a printed document, because although it could be stolen, it needs to be inserted into a device before it can be read.

Without ***physical security***, other, more sophisticated types of cyber defense become less relevant. If someone can physically get to my memory card, he or she can still steal or destroy the physical item.

***physical security*** *– measures designed to deter, prevent, detect or alert unauthorized real-world access to a site or material item.*

The same thing can happen with any critical part of my digital landscape. If someone can gain physical access to part of my digital landscape, he or she can cause disruption, steal it, or use it to gain access to even more areas.

I recall auditing a research site. The main facility where over 100 people worked was in a physically secure office space. The entire building's network, on the other hand, was managed in an unlocked cupboard, propped open by a cardboard box (to keep the cupboard cool) in the main, open and unmanned lobby.

Anybody could have walked in off the street, unchallenged, and could have pulled out 2 wires and stopped all 100 people from working. This individual could also have plugged something into the network and would thus have easily defeated all the technical defenses that were in place at that location.

Almost all ***technical controls*** are ineffective if physical access can be gained to restricted equipment.

If we return to our memory card example, if I encoded (encrypted) the information on the card, that would be an example of a technical security control. I would have done something electronically to secure the item. It might not prevent the theft of the item but it could prevent the information from being exposed.

***technical control*** *– the use of an electronic or digital method to influence or command how something like a* **digital device** *can or cannot be used. For example, removing the ability to cut or paste information on a smartphone is an example of a technical control that can be used to minimize security risks.*

The next control type to consider is procedural.

***procedural control*** *– an instruction during a sequence of required steps to limit how something is or is not permitted to be used.*

An example of a procedural control is to require a minimum of 2 authorized people to approve any access request. Procedural controls use any process (enforced or otherwise) whose purpose is to help strengthen a security position.

The last category can be referred to as legal, regulatory or compliance controls.

***legal control*** *– the use of legislation to help promote and invest in positive security methods and also to deter, punish and correct infringements.*

Whenever you hear about a large financial penalty being imposed on an organization, this is an example of the consequences of not meeting a legal control requirement.

Many companies seek to pass some of their legal financial responsibilities onto their employees or suppliers as an incentive to promote good practices. It is also normal for any breach in legal controls to result in disciplinary action.

We have only covered these 4 areas very briefly. But it is important to understand that any effective cybersecurity approach must be effective in all four control areas.

Maintaining technical controls alone will not result in effective cybersecurity.

Each time a new type of information is identified, the assets and mechanisms it will travel through also have to be identified. Any additional security protection requirements for those assets can then be consistently identified and implemented.

However, technologies and services are often deployed without the right controls and protection. To cope with this issue, we cannot rely on protection alone. Our cyber framework must also be able to actively detect and respond to these situations.

## Detect, Respond and Recover

There is a full chapter later on where we will cover the process of responding to security incidents. For now, it is useful to understand how the steps of detecting, responding and recovering fit into the overall framework.

As already mentioned, security is a lot cheaper when it is successfully achieved through proactive protection measures. That said, we still need safety nets to help identify anything that changes or slips through security controls.

Putting these safety nets in place usually includes incorporating technologies and processes that help monitor and detect potential security issues.

### Control Modes

Imagine that I want to protect my own smartphone.

There are 3 basic ways to protect my phone:

1) I can proactively take precautions that should **prevent** it from being compromised.
2) I could add mechanisms to help **detect** if it is being compromised.
3) If I later become aware of any gaps in my defenses, I might be able to reactively **correct** and address any resulting problems.

So I can use:

- ***Preventive controls***
  To protect the device **before** an event happens.
- ***Detective controls***
  To monitor and alert me in the event something happens.
- ***Corrective controls***
  To rectify any gaps **after** the problem has been identified.

In cases in which I am smart enough to be aware of a gap I can proactively fix, I can use a preventive control up front as part of the protective stage.

I can also set up methods of helping to detect anything unusual, just in case I missed something. During the detective stage, I would need to ensure that any alerts were operationally monitored so as to trigger the correct responses.

If I did miss anything, detection could possibly help to identify the need to go back and address the issue later, but in our example, this could be after I had already lost a phone!

What you should notice is that these are all time-based definitions that are called ***control modes***.

***control modes*** *- an umbrella term for preventive, detective and corrective methods of defense. Each of these methods represents a different time posture.* ***Preventive controls*** *are designed to stop an attack before it is successful,* ***detective controls*** *are designed to monitor and raise an alert during a potential compromise and* ***corrective controls*** *are the rectification of an issue after an event.*

What I do in advance is preventive, what I do during is detective and what I do after a problem occurs is corrective.

Just like any other security, cybersecurity uses all 3 of these methods to help protect digital devices from being compromised.

In an ideal world, we would be aware of all the ways in which our phones might be compromised and would be able to implement enough preventive controls to stop anything from happening. In the real world, we don't know enough to rely solely on preventive controls.

## Repeat and Refine

Since both technology and threats are changing so fast, it is important that cybersecurity itself is designed to be dynamic so it can adapt to these changes.

For this reason, outstanding cybersecurity includes efficient and repeatable processes to ensure that all the steps detailed above are triggered whenever a new technology or information asset is introduced. Optimum cybersecurity also mandates that the processes are repeated regularly.

An environment with robust security should therefore include routine 'lifecycle' repetitions that encompass both initial security measures and later re-evaluations and updates. This means that the cybersecurity team ensures that appropriate security is applied to any set of information and the assets it flows through from the outset - and that these measures are re-visited and updated on a regular basis (perhaps annually), as well as anytime there is a change or upgrade.

These repetitive measures are not just advantageous for an organization's security posture; they are also necessary for insurance and legal purposes. Cyber insurance policies are not valid (will not pay out) unless the insured company proves that these steps were carried out, and laws such as the European General Data Protection Regulation (GDPR), which governs the personal information of EU citizens, also requires proof of compliance.

If an organization cannot prove that it routinely identified its assets of value, ensured that any protective measures were appropriate to the value of the assets, and detected and addressed any significant gaps, it will find itself with 2 problems: (1) the assets will be vulnerable to cyber attack and (2) the organization will be blamed for any vulnerabilities that resulted from its failure to run its cybersecurity processes effectively.

## Defense in Depth

We have covered a lot of information in this chapter.

- The need to classify information, so we know what to protect.

- The need to understand where that information flows through, so we know where to protect.
- An introduction to the range of security control types open to us, so we know cybersecurity is not just about technical and proactive methods of protection.

Earlier in the book we mentioned and defined 'Defense-in-Depth.' This is a good time to revisit that topic.

It is always easier to mount an effective attack than to put together an effective defense. An effective defense requires the defender to adequately protect everything. An effective attack potentially only requires the attacker to find a single vulnerability.

For that reason, cybersecurity for the digital landscape requires multiple layers, checks and balances to be effective.

The larger the territory and the more assets I have within it, the more complex my cybersecurity challenge will be. That is because a vast digital landscape makes it easier for vulnerabilities to appear and remain undetected.

However, root cause analysis of widely-known cybersecurity losses has repeatedly shown that megabreaches can only occur when three or more critical or major security controls that should be in place are either missing or inadequate.

Great information security is still a foundation that we need to apply before we can hope to achieve great cybersecurity. In other words, it is still necessary to take the same basic, initial security steps in cybersecurity that we would carry out in traditional information security models that have existed for many years.

Although modern cybersecurity departments deal with highly-sophisticated attack patterns such as those seen in ***advanced persistent threats*** (APTs), the need to follow these basic approaches remains valid.

***Advanced Persistent Threats* (APTs)*** *– a term used to describe the tenacious and highly evolved set of tactics used by hackers to infiltrate networks through* ***digital devices*** *and to then leave malicious software in place for as long as possible.*

Chapter 8 will cover APTs and technical controls in more detail. However, as indicated by the case studies, most of the really large breaches happen not because there are no defenses, but because there are very often ways around those defenses.

If a cybersecurity team truly follows a defense-in-depth strategy and uses the full set of security strategies and layers, it will be almost impossible for the emergence of a single technical issue to create a cybersecurity disaster.

Also remember that security controls are only effective when they are operational and enforceable, and that the most cost-efficient way to protect any digital landscape is to embed great security by design from the very beginning. Adding security later on is a lot more expensive.

Security is not a paint that can be easily applied later on. Adding security later on is equivalent to trying to add different foundations and walls to a building after it has been built.

In summary, our basic cybersecurity model has the following proactive and reactive components:

<table>
<tr><th colspan="3">Security by Design</th></tr>
<tr><td colspan="3"></td></tr>
<tr><td rowspan="2">Proactive</td><td>√ Identify</td><td rowspan="2">Defense by Design</td></tr>
<tr><td>√ Protect</td></tr>
<tr><td rowspan="3">Reactive</td><td>√ Detect</td><td rowspan="3">Protection from Detection</td></tr>
<tr><td>√ Respond</td></tr>
<tr><td>√ Recover</td></tr>
</table>

Note that the different roles we covered in chapter 4 fit into various processes in this model; some are involved in either proactive or reactive security, and some may be involved in both categories.

One final point worth highlighting is this: it is easy to tell when an organization's cybersecurity is running badly; in such organizations, the cybersecurity department primarily relies on reactive measures and devotes a disproportionate amount of manpower to reactive approaches.

Technologies that monitor and detect intrusions are designed to be the last lines of defense. The more frequently these last lines of defense are triggered, the more obvious it becomes that the initial stages are not being run effectively or efficiently.

# 7. Human Factors

People are regarded as the weakest link in cybersecurity.

In this chapter we will aim to cover the primary ways in which human factors are frequently either the root cause or a substantial contributor to cybersecurity failures.

As part of a university lecture, I performed an analysis of the security technologies that existed in 2000, those available in the present day, and those expected to be in place by 2025. The common thread throughout was that although security improves in response to evolving threats, there remains one consistent way to bypass this security – all you have to do is compromise or misuse the valid access of an authorized user.

While it may be possible to fully secure a transaction so that only a valid, authorized person can conduct it, an attacker can still bypass these controls by simply influencing or coercing the authorized individual to perform the necessary actions on his or her behalf.

Manipulating people to do certain things is not the only human factor that can create security gaps. The most significant human factors are:

- **Inadequate cybersecurity subject knowledge** leading to the presence of large amounts of open vulnerabilities.
- **Poor capture and communication of risks** leading to repeated, unanticipated cybersecurity failures.
- **Culture and relationship issues**, both in the enterprise itself and/or in key suppliers, creating disinterested and disaffected personnel with insider knowledge.
- **Under-investment in security training** resulting in a low level of awareness about the security risks we all manage (even if we are not cybersecurity experts).
- **Using trust instead of procedures**, especially for personnel with privileged access to information, systems or devices.
- **Absence of a single point of accountability**. When more than one person is accountable, nobody is.
- **Social engineering**, which can involve various methods of leveraging insiders' access or knowledge to create opportunities that bypass other

security controls. These methods may include picking up information from personnel through traditional espionage techniques or manipulating them to do specific things.

The case studies in this book were chosen because I know from experience that they represent the same blend of factors that are typically present in the largest cybersecurity failures. It is no coincidence that each one contained a number of human factors that contributed to the cybersecurity breach.

Before we look more closely at each of these areas, I would like to share some real-world examples of how problems with human factors are easy to detect and therefore easy to take advantage of.

If an organization has poor cybersecurity, people inside and close to it know and talk about it. It is incredibly easy for a cybersecurity professional to find out how strong or weak an enterprise's cybersecurity posture is using only a few, difficult to avoid, questions in any social setting.

After a 2-day onsite security audit at a supplier's place of business, I was once asked the following question by their Chief Information Security Officer:

'We had a full, month-long internal audit a short time ago. They sent 3 people in for nearly 6 weeks. What I would like to ask is this. You were here, alone, for just over 2 days and you not only found everything they did but also some valid items that they missed. We could have saved ourselves a lot of time and money. But what I want to know is – How did you do it?'

I thought for a few seconds about whether or not to reveal the secret. I decided that with the audit over, I could.

'Body language,' I replied.

I had my full list of checks to go through, but 2 days never allowed me much time to test many of them in any depth. I would run through the checks in interview-style meetings with company personnel, and the second the body language around the table showed signs of discomfort, I knew to dig.

The larger the group of people that the company brought along to the meeting, the easier the audit became. I recall that one audit in the Philippines held the record for the most attendees; partly, I think, due to the contract size involved, they brought 28 people to the audit room.

In fact, there was a larger secret I had not revealed. Culture. In organizations with a positive culture that focuses on bettering the staff, people tend to like each other more and get along better. If a problem emerges in such companies, people bring it up and sort it out. Organizations with an employee-oriented culture that values effective teamwork tend to have fewer security gaps and problems.

I was also able to assess and test the effects of organizational culture on cybersecurity in reverse, since I was often called in to audit an organization after some kind of significant failure. In all cases, without exception, there were significant, contributing human factors that resulted from a negative culture. The security gaps often resulted from factors as simple as placing too much work on to too few people, creating stress, or bypassing, ignoring or just not putting security controls in place.

### Inadequate cybersecurity subject knowledge

Although cybersecurity relies on some traditional security principles, it also has many new requirements. The speed at which emerging technologies are adopted continuously creates more potential cybersecurity vulnerabilities.

It is not humanly possible to stay on top of the emerging threats and attack vectors unless you dedicate a substantial amount of time to continuous learning.

As a cybersecurity management specialist, I spend around 30% of my professional time reading and learning about new technologies and threats. Although this allows me to keep up with the main risks, there are frequent occasions when I have to go and research a new technology or threat type.

Cybersecurity is not a static discipline that can be learned and applied for years. An ongoing and substantial personal investment is required to stay on top of the subject area.

If a manager does not require his or her cybersecurity staff to hold and maintain current certifications from a recognized authority, he or she will inevitably have issues with the staff's level of cybersecurity knowledge.

The only thing more dangerous than training a cybersecurity employee who may then leave is not training the employee and having him or her stay.

One of the most frequent mistakes I have witnessed between 2015 and 2017 is that many organizations have a tendency to employ a small number of very high cost specialists and then deprive them of the necessary training time to keep their knowledge current.

## Poor capture and communication of risks

Chapter 12 is dedicated to this important subject area. There are, however, human factors to consider in any discussion of how risks are captured and communicated.

People often notice risks that can create substantial damage to an organization, but do not report them. This usually happens for any of three reasons:

1) The risk does not directly impact the person's immediate location, department or budget. This is an example of *silo thinking*.
2) There are sometimes negative personal or career consequences for reporting risks. Some enterprises believe that formal procedures for reporting risks conflict with the organization's risk appetite. Employees then reason that if there are no easy mechanisms or rewards for reporting suspected risks, why do it?**
3) If the process for filtering and escalating risks is not very well developed, the recipient of any reported risk information may be more inclined to bury it than to communicate and manage it.

Any organization that actively encourages its staff to identify and report risks into a structured, formal risk management framework will create a more informed and less vulnerable enterprise.

** *The topic in the second bullet above is central to another book of mine, 'Cybersecurity Exposed: The Cyber House Rules'.*

## Culture and relationship issues

Many cybersecurity threats are created from within. A corporate culture that creates disaffected or disinterested staff is much more likely to lead to this type of threat than one that fosters employee satisfaction.

In your organization, do people generally like each other, get along nicely and believe that the company invests in them and considers them to be more than assets with id numbers?

When people feel no connection to or support from their organization, they are more likely to seek opportunities to take personal advantage of their position. This is because these individuals often seek to retaliate for the lack of support they receive from the employer.

An organization's whistleblowing process is another factor that reflects the enterprise's culture and also impacts its cybersecurity posture. There are many cybersecurity failures that might have been prevented if company employees and contractors felt comfortable reporting deficiencies through an independent reporting structure that would safeguard their position and anonymity. However, in the real world, the reported issues often end up back with the people that are causing them, together with enough information to identify who reported the problem.

The more open and supportive an organization is toward its people, the more the people will reciprocate. A closed and unsupportive organization will create vulnerabilities through general disinterest from its employees and from rogue insiders who feel justified in using their knowledge and access for personal gain.

It is much easier for a cybersecurity attack to succeed with the help of an insider. An insider does not even need to have privileged access to be capable of providing significant intelligence for a cyber attack. If I have a five minute conversation with a standard employee who is disgruntled, I can usually identify enough security vulnerabilities to identify a cyber attack option. Just imagine what an insider can do if they are motivated.

Never underestimate the extent to which an enterprise's culture correlates with its security posture.

In my own experience, an enterprise with a negative culture will be riddled with security gaps and people ready to help expose them.

### Under-investment in security training

Does anybody reading this book maintain a separate username and password for every different web account they use? In a cybersecurity lecture I recently attended at the Royal Institution in London that was packed full of security specialists, about 20% of the hands went into the air.

'325 and counting,' said one person.

Whenever a cybersecurity attack succeeds in obtaining username and password details, one of the first things the criminals are likely to do is to use automated tools to try to re-use the same credentials on all the major web services. But as the cybersecurity lecture statistics reveal, many people, including cybersecurity specialists, are not aware of the importance of using different usernames and passwords for different accounts.

This underscores the greater issue that employees, suppliers and even customers need to be aware of how their actions can create, deter and detect security issues. This fact is deeply relevant to cybersecurity.

When people have access to an organization's digital systems, their actions can affect employees, customers and others as well. This is why anyone with access needs practical and regular awareness training on what the potential security threats are, how to avoid them and how to report any suspected or confirmed security problems.

Security awareness and advice needs to include specific and practical content about security threats to any relevant electronic information or systems to which a person may have access. For example:

- Do not leave your computer or mobile device unlocked when you are not with it and using it.
- Never mix alcohol with using any digital device (phone, tablet or computer) that can access systems at your workplace.
- Never discuss or speak about work when intoxicated.
- Be aware that malicious software can be loaded onto your computer, phone or tablet simply by clicking on a link. For that reason, do not click on any link that you believe may not be safe.

Good security awareness training should be concise, relevant, useful, thought-provoking and frequent. Its content also needs to be updated regularly, meaning at least once per year.

Cybersecurity is not a purely technical problem for the technical team. People are more likely to create cybersecurity failures than technology is. Security awareness is the primary way to make this known.

### Using trust instead of procedures

As a species, we tend to use failure as a learning mechanism. Only after something goes wrong do we tend to fix it.

*In many organizations, especially in those that are growing, a few select individuals enjoy unbridled privileges and are considered to be completely trustworthy. They have always been there, they have always done the right thing and to add in procedures that move away from the trust system can seem both expensive and unnecessary.*

What I have written in the paragraph above is the usual explanation that is used just after an organization was badly burned because trusting an insider proved to be a huge mistake.

Edward Snowden is a great example of this problem. He had worked as a safe pair of hands in government security for years. What could possibly go wrong?

At any point in any process that includes any type of associated privilege, it is essential that procedures are in place to ensure that no one can independently execute an action based on trust alone.

Even if a person is a Chief Information Security Officer (in fact, especially if he or she is), it should not be possible for him or her to directly control and access the security infrastructure he or she is assigned to protect.

The stringency and breadth of procedures that control and monitor access and privilege should always be proportionate to the sensitivity of the assets. The more sensitive the permissions and assets, the greater the need for additional measures to monitor, review, check and approve the actions.

### Absence of a single point of accountability

Another cornerstone of security involves ensuring that all aspects of a digital environment that require control and management have a single point of accountability.

> ***single point (of) accountability*** *(SPA or SPOA) – the principle that all critical* ***assets,*** *processes and actions must have clear ownership and traceability to a single person. The rationale is that the absence of a defined, single owner is a frequent cause of process or asset protection failure. Shared ownership is regarded as a significant security gap due to the consistent demonstration that security flaws have an increased probability of persisting when more than one person is accountable.*

Using a single point of accountability has been demonstrated to work incredibly well; it is proved to help control highly regulated systems successfully.

Shared accountability, on the other hand, does not work well. Whenever more than one person assumes ownership and responsibility for certain assets, processes, and actions, the accountability is unclear. In the event of failure, instead of being equally accountable, shared owners expect to be equally unaccountable.

Because of the complex nature of modern organizations, the roles and responsibilities of different owners sometimes overlap, but it's important for decision-makers to prevent this from happening by creating clearly-defined, non-overlapping boundaries.

For example, imagine that I own a system and you own a process that maintains it. Well-defined accountability boundaries would specify that if your process causes my system to break, the resulting defects and the costs and consequences of failure are your responsibility, while the repair of the system and recovery of costs from you are my responsibility.

## Social Engineering

One social encounter can compromise the best cybersecurity in the world. Social engineering (traditional espionage and more) is the most fascinating of the human factors.

***social engineering**** *- is the art of manipulating people through personal interaction to gain* ***unauthorized access*** *to something.*

It constantly surprises me that it is so much easier to steal information by exploiting social situations than through direct attack.

If you put on a boiler suit with a logo, carry a clipboard and have a sense of confidence, you can physically access a lot of sites that you should not be able to access. However, most social engineering that can impact cybersecurity is far less risky.

An attack team that blends espionage and geek is very effective. Unfortunately, it is very easy for such a team to intentionally place agents in situations in which they can get close enough to 'trusted' people, or can worm their way inside trusted suppliers premises or systems to extract very sensitive information.

Whenever anyone develops a friendship with someone else, he or she will have a propensity to disclose and discuss information – including information about the workplace. A small amount of insider knowledge divulged during such conversations, even from a non-technical person, can easily give a surreptitious attacker enough ammunition to bypass many layers of security.

The main protection against social engineering is through awareness training, with real life examples. Here is an example:

Bob worked as the only security guard in the main lobby of a building with 1,000 employees. The access control gate was too slow to operate in the mornings, so instead, Bob had to individually buzz the gate open for each employee. Security had become relaxed, and people were used to greeting Bob with a 'Hey Bob,' followed by Bob buzzing them in. It was clear from the look on Bob's face that he probably had no idea who most of them were. Perhaps he knew a few hundred of them.

Here are my social engineering questions:

- If I told you this story in a bar and divulged where I worked, do you think you could get into my building?
- If you visited the lobby once for a legitimate reason, do you think you might have noticed this security gap?

Many cybersecurity attacks are crimes of opportunity. Social engineering attacks are also not always premeditated. If the wrong information is passed to the wrong person at the wrong time, the opportunity can facilitate the attack.

As part of any defense-in-depth strategy, it is essential to consider that human factors are the most likely to create the opportunities that lead to a cybersecurity failure.

If you are a cybersecurity professional and ever get the chance, add a question on human factors to the root cause analysis section of any incident response procedure. Something like this:

Were any of the following human factors identified as contributing toward the security failure?

- Gaps in the procedures that should have been in place.
- Risks that were known to some but not reported or managed effectively.
- Disinterested or disaffected personnel.
- A lack of security awareness by any of the people involved.
- A level of access privilege that was not adequately monitored or segregated.
- Any form of social manipulation or fiction by an individual to gain access to information or systems.

There are, of course, another set of human factors to consider – the profile and philosophy of the people who instigate cyber attacks. These factors are considered in Chapter 11: The Cybersecurity Cold War.

Before we discuss who initiates and perpetrates cyber attacks, we need to complete our understanding of cyber defense. To do that, we now need to cover the central core of cyber defense.

# 8. Technical Cybersecurity

In this chapter, we cover what was referred to earlier as technical controls, using a six-step approach:

- What is an attack surface?
- The lifecycle of a standard cybersecurity attack.
- Basic methods of technical defense.
- Evolving methods of attack (***vectors***).
- More advanced methods of defense.
- Other methods of cyber attack and defense.

As we have progressed through the book, a lot of technical terms have slowly been introduced. In this chapter, the first time we use a technical term that has already been defined earlier in the book it will be highlighted in bold and italic text. You can then refer to the dictionary at the back of the book if you need to refresh your understanding of the meaning.

If we introduce a new technical term for the first time, we will define it directly under the paragraph where it is first used.

Many cybersecurity courses and certifications focus almost entirely on technical controls. That is a valid approach if you only need to acquire a limited, additional set of technical skills. For example, an existing information security professional would already be familiar with many of the security controls that were covered earlier in this book.

It is important to remember that even the best technical controls can still be completely circumvented by non-technical means.

Technical controls are critical to cybersecurity, but so are other non-technical layers of defense.

Defense in depth cannot be achieved without using all the security control methods, including technical, physical, procedural and others.

Remember: An effective defense requires a comprehensive approach. A successful attack can happen through a single vulnerability.

## What is an Attack Surface?

For a cyber attack to be successful, the first thing the attacker needs to achieve is a point of entry.

When defending a digital landscape, we need to understand which area(s) the attackers could target. This target area is referred to as the ***attack surface***.

***attack surface**** *– the sum of the different points where an unauthorized user (the "attacker") can try to enter **data** into or extract data from an environment.*

Back in chapter six we looked at ***cyber defense points*** and identified six major categories:

*i)* ***Data*** *– any information in electronic or digital format.*
*ii)* ***Devices*** *– any hardware used to create, modify, process, store or transmit **data**. Computers, smartphones and USB drives are all examples of devices.*
*iii)* ***Applications*** *– any programs (software) that reside on any **device**. Usually programs exist to create, modify, process, store, inspect or transmit specific types of data.*
*iv)* ***Systems*** *– groups of **applications** that operate together to serve a more complex purpose.*
*v)* ***Networks*** *– the group name for a collection of devices, wiring and applications used to connect, carry, broadcast, monitor or safeguard data. Networks can be physical (use material assets such as wiring) or virtual (use applications to create associations and connections between devices or applications.)*
*vi)* *Other **communication channels** – used to send, store or receive electronic information.*

If any item from the list above carries or handles information for an enterprise, it will be part of the potential attack surface.

Even if an application exists within a supplier's digital systems, if it contains the enterprise's data or provides critical services, any consequences of a successful cyber attack will usually still be the organization's legal responsibility. This means that it is critical to remember to include these external parts when considering the attack surface.

The enterprise may not be responsible for operating these external systems day to day, but it is still responsible for ensuring the correct security is in place and is also accountable if the security fails to protect its own services or information.

Part of the role of the security architect is to try to reduce the size of the attack surface while also sustaining ongoing business needs. Any time the size and complexity of the attack surface can be reduced, it becomes easier to defend.

Another method of reducing the security risk is to subdivide the attack surface. This can be achieved using ***network segmentation***, which gives the system greater resilience.

> **network segmentation** – *splitting a single collection of* ***devices,*** *wiring and* ***applications*** *that connect, carry, broadcast, monitor or safeguard* ***data*** *into smaller sections. This allows for more discrete management of each section, allowing greater security to be applied in sections with the highest value, and also permitting smaller sections to be impacted in the event of a* ***malware*** *infection or other disruptive event.*

If one segment is attacked or otherwise compromised, it can be isolated with less overall impact to the full digital landscape used by the organization.

In addition, it is possible to create different security zones. Higher levels of security can then be applied to attack surfaces (including network segments) in which higher-value data is stored or transacted. Lower (and less costly) levels of security can be used where the information stored or transacted is itself of low value.

Care must be taken when evaluating where lower levels of security can be permitted. This is because there are frequent examples of attack exploits that have used low security areas of an attack surface as an access route to higher security areas. Remember Edward Snowden? He simply found a document that had been incorrectly classified at a lower security level to provide a map that allowed him to take information from much more tightly secured parts of the digital landscape.

### The Lifecycle of a Cybersecurity Attack

Most cyber attacks involve ***malware***. If malware is involved, there are usually seven basic stages to the attack process. These are:

- (i) Reconnaissance
- (ii) Tooling / preparation

(iii) Infection
(iv) Persistence
(v) Communication
(vi) Control
(vii) Realizing the value

This lifecycle is usually described as an ***advanced persistent threat***, also known as an ***APT***. APTs are defined earlier in the book, and a fuller definition can also be found in the terminology section.

We will now look at each stage of the lifecycle in more detail.

<u>Reconnaissance</u>

To make an attack as cost-efficient for the criminals as possible, nothing beats research. The Internet is a vast repository of information for cyber attackers.

There are tools (Harvester is one) that allow people to simply type in the website name of a potential target and the program reveals all the names, email addresses, job titles and other information that the organization's staff have placed on public sites such as LinkedIn, Facebook and others.

You may also recall that the Target (retailer) hack is alleged to have used a publicly available diagram detailing how its point of sales system was configured.

For a more targeted attack, especially by nation states, hanging out at a local bar or networking at conferences can also be a great way of acquiring intelligence about the easiest routes to compromise an environment, especially if the reconnaissance specialists can find the disgruntled employees or consultants.

<u>Tooling / preparation</u>

Equipped with an understanding of potential routes into an environment and systems to target, the hacker can now put together the right tools for the job.

Hacking no longer requires extensive technical knowledge. Malware can now be assembled as easily as a Word document can be prepared. Readily available software allows custom malware to be put together by just clicking the desired capabilities, and then the hacker can add his or her own unique encryption.

More advanced malware creation tools will even let hackers define how they want their attack tools to change their appearance - and how often - to help them avoid detection.

Infection

During the ***infection*** stage, the attacker seeks to use any method possible to place malware into any part of the target attack surface.

***infection*** – *(in the context of **cybersecurity**) unwanted invasion by an outside agent that an attacker uses to create damage or disruption.*

Persistence

Once in place, the malware will try to persist by using as many opportunities as it can to bypass or disable defenses, copy itself into locations where it can re-install whenever an asset is reset or restored, and disguise itself as an inconspicuous file.

Seeking to remain in place within the attack surface is referred to as ***persistence***. A frequent target for helping malware persist is to install it into the ***master boot record***.

***persistence*** – *to seek continued existence despite opposition.*

***master boot record*** – *the first sector on any electronic **device** that defines which operating **system** should be loaded when it is initialized or re-started.*

Installing on the master boot record allows the malware to re-install itself when a device is re-started. This offers the potential to disable or bypass other security measures that may be commenced during the start-up (or 'boot') sequence.

Often the malware will use an ***exploit*** known as a ***buffer overflow*** (intentionally writing more data to the memory than is possible) to achieve command-level access known as ***shell access***.

***exploit*** – *to take advantage of a security **vulnerability**.*

***buffer overflow*** – *exceeding the region of electronic memory used to temporarily store **data** when it is being moved between locations. This process is used by some forms of **malware** to **exploit** an electronic target.*

***shell access*** – *command-level permission to perform executive control over an electronic **device**.*

Communication

To be effective, malware usually needs the ability to communicate. Communication (inbound and outbound) can allow malware to do one or more of the following:

- Find other malware with which to cooperate.
- ***Exfiltrate*** stolen information.
- Take instruction from the attack controller (for example - from a ***bot herder***).

***bot herder*** *- is a* ***hacker*** *who uses automated techniques to seek vulnerable* ***networks*** *and* ***systems.*** *The bot herder's initial goal is to install or find* ***bot*** *programs that can be used to achieve a particular purpose. Once one or more bots are in place, the hacker can control these programs to perform a larger objective of stealing, corrupting and/or disrupting information,* ***assets*** *and services. See also* ***botnet.***

***bot*** *- is a computer program designed to perform specific tasks. They are usually simple, small and designed to perform fast, repetitive tasks. When the purpose of the program conflicts with an organization's goals and needs, a bot can be considered to be a form of* ***malware.*** *See also* ***botnet.***

If malware can communicate, it can often be remotely adapted to change or add functions and can even receive updates (new programming) that allow it to continue to avoid damage or to take even greater advantage of the infiltration point it has penetrated.

Each piece of malware often has multiple communication options. If one communication method is ineffective, it can switch to another. It can also receive updates about new communication paths, or, if it can find other familiar malware, it can potentially use that for its own communication purposes.

Attackers usually seek to install or leverage large numbers of bots, which results in a ro**bot**ic **net**work referred to as a **botnet**. This provides greater resiliency to the attack, plus offers a greater number of potential communication channels.

Control

Once malware is in place and is persisting and communicating, the attacker can then coordinate, update and direct what the malware does.

If defensive measures can prevent malware from communicating with the controller, it often becomes harmless, since losing the ability to receive instructions or to send out stolen information usually renders it ineffective.

Some forms of cyber defense use ***decapitation*** as one method of stopping malware after it has been discovered.

> **Decapitation*** – *(in the context of* **malware***) preventing any compromised* **device** *from being able to communicate, receive instruction, send information or spread malware to other devices. This can effectively render many forms of malware ineffective because it removes any command, control or theft benefit. This is often a stage during* **threat** *removal.*

Realizing the value

No cyber attack is worthwhile unless the perpetrator derives some value from it.

That value may simply be to disrupt operations, steal and resell information or demand a ransom.

An attack only becomes truly worthwhile to an attacker when he or she gets the payoff. If he or she performs a ***ransomware*** attack but fails to collect a ransom payment, it may cost the target organization a lot of time and money, but it will still result in a net loss for the criminals. For that reason, regardless of the interruption in communications or other services that results, **it is never advisable for any organization or individual to ever pay in response to any ransomware demand.**

> **ransomware** *– a form of malicious software (***malware***) that prevents or restricts usage of one or more* **digital devices** *or* **applications** *or renders a collection of electronic* **data** *unreadable until a sum of money is paid.*

### Basic Methods of Technical Defense

For each part of the attack surface (also known as the cyber defense points), there are a range of options that can be used to prevent or detect a cyber attack.

It takes considerably more effort to manage a cyber attack once an infection has successfully settled in. Indeed, once an attacker has gained ***unauthorized access***, the malware can often persist for months or even years.

It is more effective to prevent infection or intrusion than it is to take corrective measures afterwards.

In the early days of technical protection, most attacks were launched through email. This is no longer the case. Attackers now use any vector (method of attack) they can. The evolving techniques are covered in the next part of this chapter.

Attacks can occur anywhere on an attack surface, so it is important to consider the primary methods of defense and where they can be deployed. Remember, the key components of an attack surface are:

- Data
- Networks
- Devices
- Applications
- Systems
- Other communication channels

We should also define the difference between ***host-based*** and ***network-based*** defenses.

***host-based*** *– describes a situation in which something is installed immediately on the* ***device*** *it is protecting, servicing or subverting.*

***network-based*** *– describes a situation in which something is installed to protect, serve or subvert the community of* ***devices****, wiring and* ***applications*** *used to connect, carry, broadcast, monitor or safeguard information (the* ***network****).*

Many years ago, it was considered sufficient to primarily rely on network-based security measures. This is no longer adequate. Enterprises now run security everywhere they can. This means every part of the attack surface should include an adequate and appropriate selection of security defenses.

Network security is no longer a reliable security defense layer for many reasons, including:

- Many activities take place away from networks (mobile and cloud applications for example).
- A network can fail to detect malware that runs through it when the malware is encrypted or is disguised as legitimate traffic.

- Networks can no longer rely on 'trust' between devices they contain, as the devices themselves are no longer capable of easily identifying and defeating attacks.

Many small businesses are now moving away from even setting up computer networks. Instead, they seek to secure each item (applications, devices, services) and to run adequate back-up and recovery processes.

There are now literally hundreds of different types of security defense technologies available. As threats emerge, so do new technologies to help address them. These technologies, when effective, are then gradually merged into simpler, more unified and easier-to-deploy software and hardware.

Because of the large number of technologies, in this section, we will only focus on some of the most established and leading forms.

The primary technical methods of defense can be considered to be:

- Anti-malware / advanced endpoint protection solutions
- Firewalls
- Intrusion Prevention & Intrusion Detection
- Data Loss Prevention
- Encryption / cryptography (although this is also used for attack)
- Proxy servers (again, also used for both attack and defense)
- Identity and Access Controls
- Containerization and virtualization
- Penetration testing
- Vulnerability assessment

We will now provide a basic definition for each of these primary, technical security controls.

***endpoint*** *– any electronic device that can be used to store or process information. Laptops, smartphones and even smart watches are all examples of an endpoint.*

<u>Anti-malware</u>

***anti-malware*** *– is a computer program designed to look for specific files and behaviors (****signatures****) that indicate the presence or the attempted installation of malicious software. If or when detected, the program seeks to isolate the* ***attack***

*(quarantine or block the* ***malware****), remove it, if it can, and also alert appropriate people to the attempt or to the presence of the malware. The program can be* ***host-based*** *(installed on* ***devices*** *that are directly used by people) or* ***network-based*** *(installed on gateway devices through which information is passed). Older forms of this software could detect only specific, pre-defined forms of malicious software using signature files. Newer forms use* ***machine learning*** *and make use of additional techniques including* ***behavior monitoring****.*

***signatures*** *- (in the context of* ***cybersecurity****) are the unique attributes - for example, file size, file extension,* ***data*** *usage patterns and method of operation - that identify a specific computer program. Traditional* ***anti-malware*** *and other security technologies can make use of this information to identify and manage some forms of rogue software or communications.*

*Further definitions for bolded terms in this section can be found in the Cybersecurity to English section of this book.*

Anti-malware is a primary method of defense. To be effective, it is usually installed on as many different parts of the attack surface as possible. This will usually include user devices (computers, smartphones, tablets, ...) and network hardware.

The anti-malware market is undergoing an evolution. It used to be difficult to create malware. When that was true, anti-malware relied on teams of people to analyze anything new and write specific identification and isolation routines that would block and quarantine harmful programs.

That process is no longer effective. A new generation of anti-malware now relies on the ability to recognize suspected malware using a basic form of artificial intelligence. A file no longer has to even be run before it can be isolated or removed. This 'nextgen' (next generation) anti-malware can block over 99% of malware, even if the suspect program has never before been encountered.

Unfortunately, many established customers still use older forms of anti-malware that are largely ineffective. So if you are an individual or work for a company with older anti-malware in place, it is a good idea to check on how well it runs and how effective it claims to be against new, modified and previously unknown malware. Organizations with nextgen anti-malware have substantially fewer problems to clean up.

More advanced applications and systems may also have their own, additional anti-malware that operates during certain functions; for example, it may scan uploaded files for threats before allowing the user to store, read or otherwise use the files. This is particularly important because applications and systems may use forms of encryption that can bypass other security defenses by masquerading as application data.

Anti-malware needs to be regularly updated with the latest updates that contain information about new and evolved threats.

Firewalls

***firewall*** *– is hardware (physical device) or software (computer program) used to monitor and protect inbound and outbound* ***data*** *(electronic information). It achieves this by applying a set of rules. These physical* ***devices*** *or computer programs are usually deployed, at a minimum, at the perimeter of each* ***network*** *access point. Software firewalls can also be deployed on devices to add further security. The rules applied within a firewall are known as the* ***firewall policy.*** *Advanced firewalls are often equipped with other defensive features typical of more* ***unified threat management.***

Firewalls act as gatekeepers at the borders of each network and on devices as well.

Early firewalls relied mainly on understanding the sender's ***Internet protocol (IP)*** address, the destination ***port number*** and the ***protocol*** (method of communication) being used.

***protocol*** *- (in the context of electronic communications) is a set of established rules used to send information between different electronic locations. Protocols provide a standard that can be used to send or receive information in an expected and understandable format, including information about the source, destination and route. Examples of protocols include* ***Internet protocol*** *(IP),* ***hyper text transfer protocol*** *(HTTP),* ***file transfer protocol*** *(FTP),* ***transmission control protocol*** *(TCP),* ***border gateway protocol*** *(BGP) and* ***dynamic host configuration protocol*** *(DHCP).*

***Internet Protocol*** *- is the set of rules used to send or receive information from or to a location on a* ***network,*** *including information about the source, destination and route. Each electronic location (host) has a unique address (the* ***IP address****) that is used to define the source and the destination.*

***port number*** *- used as part of an electronic communication to denote the method of communication being used. This allows the* ***packet*** *to be directed to a program that will know what to do with it.*

***packet*** *- (in the context of electronic communication) is a bundle of electronic information grouped together for transmission. The bundle usually includes control information to indicate the destination, source and type of content, and the content (user information) itself.*

The allowable and prohibited values were stored as the firewall policy in these early firewalls. This setup was known as a ***packet-filtering*** approach. It allowed for fast throughput but did not inspect the content of the packets. This made it vulnerable to ***spoofing***.

***packet-filtering**** *- passing or blocking bundles of electronic information based on rules. See also* ***packet***.

***spoofing*** *- concealing the true source of electronic information by impersonation or other means. Often used to bypass Internet security filters by pretending the source is from a trusted location.*

In addition to packet-filtering and port blocking, firewalls now include additional defenses, including ***intrusion prevention, intrusion detection*** and other methods that are explained below.

Strong firewalls also include a good firewall policy, which can usually be recognized by virtue of the fact that it contains only a small number of rules and also displays evidence of being reviewed frequently to ensure it remains configured to guard against the latest threats.

Intrusion Prevention and Intrusion Detection

***Intrusion Detection Systems (IDS)*** *- computer programs that monitor and inspect electronic communications that pass through them, with the purpose to detect, log (record) and raise alerts on any suspected malicious or otherwise unwanted streams of information. IDS are a variation of* ***Intrusion Detection and Prevention Systems***, *as they have no ability to block the activity; they only monitor, inspect and alert.*

***Intrusion Detection and Prevention Systems (IDPS)*** *- computer programs that* *monitor and inspect electronic communications that pass through them, with the purpose and ability (i) to block and log (record) key information about any known malicious or otherwise unwanted streams of information and (ii) to log and raise alerts about any other traffic that is suspected (but not confirmed) to be of a similar nature. These are usually placed in the communication path to allow the IDPS to prevent unwanted information from entering or leaving a* ***network*** *by dropping or blocking* ***packets****. IDPS can also clean some electronic* ***data*** *to remove any unwanted or undesirable packet components.*

***Intrusion Prevention Systems (IPS)*** *– see* ***Intrusion Detection and Prevention Systems****. A slight variation in IPS, compared to* ***IDPS****, is that they may not collect any detection information and may only serve to block (prevent) unwanted traffic based on direct rules or instructions they receive.*

Prevention is always preferable to detection alone. If an intrusion is detected after the event, then the overhead to correct the issue is greater.

There are two key challenges for these systems.

The first problem is determining what a malicious or unwanted communication looks like. This can be achieved by three different methods:

- Storing known attack communication patterns, which are known as ***signatures***. These can then be specifically detected, and (in the case of intrusion prevention), blocked.
- It is also possible for the programs to review statistics and look for any behavior that is unusual or anomalous. This form of detection is known as ***statistical anomaly-based detection***.
- Sometimes, malicious or unwanted communications adjust the packets in which they are sent so the protocol differs from its usual format. Detecting significant variations in protocol format is thus another way to identify malicious communications. This is known as ***stateful protocol analysis detection***.

The second and more significant issue is that people want their communications to be transmitted and received quickly and without interruption. Imposing numerous detection rules and frequently encountering detection and prevention systems slows down communications, so intrusion prevention and detection involves a balancing act between security and performance.

If too many rules and restrictions are in place, electronic traffic (communications) can be lost or delayed. If too few are in place, unwanted data can enter and leave without being detected or blocked.

Data Loss Prevention

***Data Loss Prevention* (DLP)*** *- is a term that describes blocking specific types of information from leaving an electronic* ***device.*** *There are dedicated types of hardware and software that can be used to facilitate this objective.*

One of the key objectives for any attacker is to steal information of value. This valuable information usually has certain attributes that can also be used to defend it.

Using these information attributes to help prevent data loss depends on various methods of bolstering security by positioning technologies in key parts of a digital landscape.

Host-based data loss prevention is one such technology that can help to stop people from sending critical, sensitive or otherwise valuable information outside an enterprise's network.

Network-based data loss prevention technologies can control the types of information that are allowed to be transmitted between locations.

It is up to the organization that is putting data loss prevention in place to define the business rules (criteria) that will be applied to permit or prevent certain types of information from traveling. ***Information classification***, covered earlier in the book, can be used in such data loss prevention security; however, advanced data loss programs can also automatically detect the presence of certain information, even if it has not been classified. Any attempts to move information against company rules can then be either blocked or challenged.

Any critical information that is permitted to travel can also be made more secure through the use of additional ***encryption*** (covered below).

Specialized data loss prevention technologies have proven particularly useful when applied directly to the devices (computers, smartphones and tablets) that people use and also on critical business applications that transact large volumes of information; for example, on email services and financial systems.

In addition to blocking the movement of data, these security programs can also raise alerts and can even insert data that helps trace the origin and destination of packets without the user's knowledge.

These technologies are also very valuable in locations where substantial personal information is transacted. They can help ensure that privacy regulations are provably enforced.

Encryption / cryptography

The art of encoding messages so that they cannot be read by anybody who intercepts them has existed for a very long time. For example, around 160 BCE the Greek historian Polybius invented and described a cryptographic technique known as the Polybius Square. The Cypher Research Laboratories in Australia describes it like this: "Messages were encoded by substituting the letter in the text by one that is three positions to the right. A became D, V became Y etc." The first person known to use this tool was Julius Caesar.

Modern cryptographic techniques are somewhat harder to decipher, but the advantages of encryption – that it is a security technique that can be applied directly to data, and that the data is just a useless jumble of characters without the ability to decrypt the information – remain valid.

Although it is very useful in helping to secure general communications, there are two major problems with encryption:

The first problem is that encrypted information is very much like carrying a diplomatic bag, or pouch. Nobody can inspect the contents unless he or she has the key or can crack open the container. That is an advantage if someone wants to prevent the information from slipping into the wrong hands, but it also means that the contents of nearly all the information streaming past an organization's other security measures cannot be inspected. This is covered further in the next chapter.

The other big problem is that encryption does not last. It works reasonably well if you want to keep something secure that is not time-sensitive. However, all encryption can eventually be broken, given enough time and resources. Encryption that is nearly impossible to decrypt today will be relatively easy to break ten years down the line.

Even with these limitations, encryption is still a vital part of a security toolset. It prevents information that is intercepted during the communications phase from being immediately vulnerable.

Automatic encryption and decryption techniques can (for example) be placed on email services to help protect messages during transmission.

Proxy servers

***proxy server*** *– is a program used to provide intermediate services between a requested transaction and its destination. Instead of sending the transaction 'as is,' it can adjust some of the information to help secure the anonymity of the sender. In addition, it may store (cache) any information that is accessed often to help speed up response times.*

The primary security role of a proxy server is to help keep information about the sender or requestor hidden or secret to prevent that information from being misused. For example, when you request a page on the Internet, instead of revealing your name and precise computer details, the proxy server can substitute other information. When the response to the request is received, it can then seamlessly direct the requested information back to you.

Proxy servers enhance security by hiding exact information about locations and users in a particular network.

Attackers also frequently use proxy servers for the same purposes.

Identity and Access Controls

***identity and access controls*** *– method(s) of regulating how each person and computer service is confirmed to be who they claim to be (authentication) and how their permissions are monitored.*

Determining whether each information transaction is legitimate is simpler when the identity of the requestor and his or her permission to do what he or she is requesting can be easily confirmed.

The greater the number of different identity and access systems that a given enterprise manages, the more likely these systems are to be attacked.

Security architects usually aim to use a single primary technology to control identity and high-level access rights across an enterprise's entire digital landscape as part of most security strategies.

This allows each person's access permissions to be easily changed or revoked. It also allows any attempts to fraudulently enter an account to be easily identified.

Each separate username and password usually indicates that a separate identity management system is being utilized. The more separate identity management systems there are, the greater the likelihood of systems being compromised without being noticed.

Secure identity management systems now use processes that even allow external systems to use a single, central username and password without the need to share password information back with the external system. For example, a cloud service can use an enterprises username and password through a connection that validates the authenticity without revealing anything more than whether or not the access attempt is valid.

Although access permissions are largely a procedural control - for example, ensuring that each person is assigned the least amount of privilege required to perform his or her duties - there is also a technical aspect.

Access rights are administered and enforced through applications and systems.

Similarly, by centrally tracking privilege levels across different systems, or by enforcing privilege restrictions from a central location, attempts to break business rules that concern access can be more easily identified.

Containerization and virtualization

With the increase in webpages and emails that contain malware, there are now many technologies that can isolate activities like Internet surfing and email management to prevent them from accidently infecting sensitive data and systems. These technologies cordon off these Internet activities so they are performed in secure environments that cannot spread malware even if they become infected.

These technologies make it possible to use a single device, but at the same time to isolate and process web surfing and email activities in such a way that it is very unlikely that any infection will affect the physical device.

These technologies use a technique called 'virtualization,' which creates an isolated software replica to replace an electronic device's real operating system, then creates, uses and deletes a new replica during each use. Even if the isolated replica acquires an infection, its configuration can prevent the malware from escaping and can then fully delete it as a matter of routine after each use. Each time a new Web surfing or email session begins, a completely new software replica of the operating environment is created and is then deleted when the session is completed.

Initially, virtualization software was sold as a separate security technology, but it is now incorporated into some operating systems and applications.

Penetration testing

***penetration test*** *(also known as an* ***attack and penetration test*** *or* ***pen. test)*** *– checks and scans on any* ***application, system*** *or website to identify any potential security gaps (****vulnerabilities****) that could be* ***exploited.*** *Once the vulnerabilities are identified, this process then goes on to identify the extent to which these vulnerabilities could be leveraged in an* ***attack*** *(the penetration possibilities). Usually these checks are performed in a test area and emulate the same techniques that could be used by an attacker. This is to prevent any inadvertent operational disruption. The checks are typically conducted before any application or site is first used, and also on a periodic (repeating) basis; for example, each time the program is updated or every 6 months. Any significant gaps must be addressed (fixed) in a timeframe appropriate to the scale of the* ***risk.*** *Not to be confused with the term* ***vulnerability assessment,*** *which only identifies gaps without examining how they could be leveraged.*

***vulnerability*** *– (in the context of* ***cybersecurity****) a weakness, usually in design, implementation or operation of software (including operating systems), that could be compromised and result in damage or harm.*

There are a significant number of potential security gaps that can be present inside each computer program. These programs are represented on an attack surface by applications and systems.

The only way to check for the presence of these vulnerabilities is through a process referred to as ***penetration testing***. This process can utilize ethical hackers that an enterprise pays to manually try to identify security weaknesses. There are also automated tools that can perform similar assessments.

***White-box*** penetration testing (also known as clear-box testing) is the term used to describe a situation in which the technical layout of the computer program being tested has been made available for the penetration test. This makes the test easier and cheaper to perform, but usually results in the identification of more issues than ***black-box testing*** identifies.

Black-box penetration testing is the term used to describe a situation in which the penetration testers are given no advance information about the computer program's technical details. Although this scenario usually reflects the characteristics of a true attack more accurately (unless the attackers manage to get a copy of the technical details), it is more expensive and usually less effective in locating all potential security vulnerabilities.

Any significant gaps identified during penetration testing (or at any other time) must be fixed. Usually, this is completed before putting a program into real-world use. If a gap is identified in a program that is already in real-world use, the corrective approach will depend on a comparison of the risks and costs that will be incurred if the vulnerability is exploited versus the costs the business would incur from an interim suspension of the program.

Vulnerability assessment

***vulnerability assessment*** *– the identification and classification of security gaps in a computer, software* ***application, network*** *or other section of a* ***digital landscape.*** *This is usually a passive identification technique that aims only to identify the gaps, without exploring how those gaps could be used in an* ***attack.*** *This should not be confused with a* ***penetration test,*** *which may include information from a* ***vulnerability*** *assessment, but which will go on to explore how any vulnerabilities can be exploited.*

***port scanning*** *– a process, usually run by computer, to detect open* ***access*** *points (ports) that could be used to infiltrate or* ***exfiltrate*** *electronic information into or out of an enterprise.*

Penetration testing is only one method of identifying vulnerabilities; indeed, there are many others. Keeping up to date with industry notifications about new vulnerabilities is one such method. Running frequent or continuous ***port scanning*** and full vulnerability assessments are two further examples.

Knowing which potential vulnerabilities exist is only part of the process. It is important to follow through and close or otherwise mitigate these potential gaps in an appropriately prioritized order.

Collectively, all of the above methods represent the most current primary methods of technical protection for electronic devices and the information they process, store and transact.

However, the speed with which we adopt new technologies means that attackers are continuously seeking new and more ingenious ways of breaching these defenses, so unfortunately they do not stay current for very long.

One major defense technique we have not yet covered is the use of security coordination programs that unify threat intelligence.

Now is a good time to look at how these threats and attacks are evolving and what we can do to counteract these new exploits.

# 9. Evolving Attack and Defense Methods

When I wrote the first edition of this book, cybersecurity was only a topic of interest to cybersecurity specialists and savvy executives. The book was written to be accessible for anyone, and although I predicted massive increases in cyber attacks, even I did not expect the rapid growth in cybercrime to be so extreme.

Cybercrime is now the fastest-growing industry on the planet, with estimated revenues of $445 billion in 2016 (source: World Economic Forum). That figure is expected to more than double in the next few years.

In the previous chapter, we reviewed the primary traditional methods of preventing and detecting cyber attacks.

The information presented about these defenses was very basic, and in this beginner's text the primary objective is to provide only a basic, overall understanding of this broad subject area. However, any discussion of the ways in which attack and defense methods are evolving requires a more in-depth look at the different technical and other types of controls. This chapter will thus take it up a notch and go into how attacks and defenses are evolving.

Firstly, as we covered in earlier chapters, the only way to effectively prevent unwanted intrusions or misuse of electronics and the information they contain is to take a more holistic approach than simply implementing technical controls allows.

As an example, the UK Cyber Essentials scheme, which is one of many frameworks designed to help organizations create better defenses, states that effective management of just five key areas will protect against 80% of attacks. These areas are:

- Effective firewall positioning and management.
- ***Secure configuration***.
- User ***access controls***.
- Malware protection.
- Timely ***patch management***.

***secure configuration*** *– ensuring that when settings are applied to any item (**device** or software), appropriate steps are always taken to ensure (i)* ***default accounts*** *are removed or disabled, (ii) shared accounts are not used and (iii) all* *protective and defensive* **controls** *in the item use the strongest appropriate setting(s).*

**default accounts** *- generic user and password permissions, often with administrative access that is provided as standard for some* **applications** *and hardware for use during initial setup.*

**access controls** *- rules and techniques used to manage and restrict entry to or exit from a physical, virtual or digital area through the use of permissions. Permissions are usually assigned individually to a person,* **device** *or* **application** *service to ensure accountability and traceability of usage. The permissions can be secured using (i) physical tokens (something you have); for example a key card, (ii) secret information (something you know); such as a password or (iii) biometric information - using part of the human body such as a fingerprint or eye scan to gain access (something you are). See also* **multi-factor authentication.**

**patch management** *- a controlled process used to deploy critical, interim updates to software on* **digital devices.** *The release of a software 'patch' is usually in response to a critical flaw or gap that has been identified. Any failure to apply new interim software updates promptly can leave open security* **vulnerabilities** *in place. As a consequence, promptly applying these updates (patch management) is considered a critical component of maintaining effective* **cybersecurity.**

What is noticeable in the list above is that the three bolded items (secure configuration, user access controls and timely patch management), rely on humans to execute certain procedures. They are thus not direct technical controls, but are process controls that need to be applied to networks, systems, devices and applications.

Back-up (regularly taking a copy of valuable information to a secure location) also often relies on setting up the right processes - and is often a key process that can allow computer systems to be restored in the event of a successful attack.

Whether the controls applied are mainly technical or rely primarily on human efforts, the case studies showed that it is never an isolated technical failure that results in increased vulnerability to cyber attacks.

For that reason, intelligent security coordination software is increasingly being used for cyber defense.

Security coordination software is designed to bring together a fuller picture of the status of different security controls. However, it is important to note that just like zooming in and out on a map, there are many different levels of coordination available.

A great way to coordinate the overall security position of an enterprise is through a central, comprehensive ***governance***, ***risk*** management and ***compliance*** system. At the highest level, an enterprise's governance, risk and compliance system is designed to pull together:

- ***Governance*** information – is the full range of policies, procedures and specific controls that the executive of an enterprise uses to keep the organization working within acceptable boundaries. This includes direct security policies, procedures and controls, and also indirect regulations that can also influence or impact security.
- ***Compliance*** information – is data that results from processes used to identify security gaps and to verify that governance regulations are being followed.
- ***Risk*** information – pertains to anything that can possibly have a substantial and material impact on the organization. This data can come from multiple sources, including gaps in compliance that have been identified, as well as new threats (such as changes in regulations or new types of exploits).

Although collecting and synchronizing this highest-level information is the best way of creating an informed picture of the overall security position, it relies on the ability to pull information from more granular sources of security coordination software. Granular sources can include the results from vulnerability assessments, penetration tests, audits, incidents and other sources of information about potential gaps and threats,

Network operations centers often pull together information about information traffic and attempts at intrusion.

Anti-malware coordination suites can monitor assets to ensure their individual anti-malware software is functioning, being updated and collecting information about attempted infection rates.

Corrective and preventive action systems can operate to measure, manage and monitor identified problems through to closure. Often, these actions are not efficiently analyzed to identify repeating patterns that can allow for more efficient remediation.

There are more than 30 different security control processes that can aggregate information. However, if they only aggregate their information in silos without an ability to understand how they relate to each other, the opportunity to understand what really needs to be prioritized is lost.

If we look at the case studies, it is usually the inability to understand the really big picture that is most likely to create sufficient gaps to allow a major breach of cyber security. Because of defense-in-depth techniques, it is unlikely that a single gap on its own will result in a major loss.

Before we look at even more defense methods, we should consider how the attacks themselves are evolving.

## Evolving Attack Methods

In the past few years, cyber attacks have increasingly involved 3 trends:

- A massive increase in the use of ransomware
- Capturing and re-using valid user and password access information
- DDoS (Distributed Denial of Service) attacks

### Ransomware

The most significant change in recent years has been the phenomenal boom in the use of ransomware. As previously defined, this is an approach that aims to directly extract money from the target being attacked by locking or encrypting the individual's or organization's files and/or devices and only releasing them in return for a ransom payment.

Of course, if you run the right security software, or even adequately back up information in an external location, ransomware is not effective. However, the majority of people and organizations lack these basic defenses.

Ransomware has been enabled by cryptocurrency, a form of anonymous payment that allows money to be transferred without an easy way of identifying the recipient.

Cyber criminals no longer have to rely on reselling stolen information to other criminals to profit from cyber crime. The ease of earning a profit from ransomware has driven the substantial increase in criminals targeting both private individuals and small businesses in this way. In fact, in most countries, cybercrime is now the most prolific form of criminal activity.

Most cyber attacks in the past relied on transmitting malware through email or by encouraging a target to download an unknown application onto a device. This is also how ransomware finds its way into digital devices.

One of the earliest techniques used (and still used) is known as ***phishing***.

> ***phishing*** *– using an electronic communication (for example email or instant messaging) that pretends to come from a legitimate source, in an attempt to get sensitive information (for example, a password or credit card number) from the recipient or to install* ***malware*** *on the recipient's* ***device****. The methods used in phishing have evolved so that the message can simply contain a link to an Internet location where malware is situated or can include an attachment (such as a PDF or Word document) that installs malware when opened. The malware can then be used to run any number of unauthorized functions, including stealing information from the device, replicating additional malware to other accessible locations, sharing the user screen, logging keyboard entries made by the user or locking out access in a ransomware attack. Less complex forms of phishing can encourage the recipient to visit a fake but convincing version of a website and to disclose passwords or other details.*

An evolved version of this technique became known as ***spear phishing***.

> ***spear phishing*** *– a more targeted form of* ***phishing****. This term describes the use of an electronic communication (for example, email or instant messaging) that targets a particular person or group of people (for example, employees at a location) and pretends to come from a legitimate source. In this case, the source may also pretend to be someone known and trusted to the recipient, in an attempt to obtain sensitive information (for example, a password or credit card number).*

Malware, such as ransomware, can also be unintentionally downloaded simply by clicking on a single Internet link. Even when the user lacks the permission to install software on a device, the malware can sometimes circumvent this control and install anyway.

To increase the chances of success, attackers often make use of major social media sites and popular web services. Facebook, Twitter, Ebay and other sites can all carry links inserted by their users. If an attacker makes the link interesting enough to entice the victim to click on it, this allows the malware to potentially gain a foothold.

Another issue is that sometimes these social media and web service sites cannot be blocked because at least some business functions require these tools to communicate or connect with customers.

These sites also use secure, encrypted protocols, such as ***SSL***, to prevent their content from being intercepted. These protocols make it difficult for typically used security devices to detect or block information, including malware, while it is being sent or received.

*SSL – is an acronym for Secure Sockets Layer. This is a method (**protocol**) for providing **encrypted** communication between two points in a **digital landscape**. For example, this could be between a **web server** (the computer hosting a web service or web site) and a **web browser** (the program that a recipient uses to view the web page; for example, Internet Explorer). In the **URL** (the Internet address visible to the user), the use of SSL is denoted by an 'https:' prefix.*

File sharing and instant messaging services can also be exploited in the same way.

This form of attack is referred to as a ***drive-by download***.

***drive-by download** – the unintended receipt of malicious software onto a **device** through an Internet page, electronic service or link. The victim is usually unaware that his or her actions permitted new malicious software to be pulled onto and installed into the **digital device** or **network**.*

Another way in which attackers make it increasingly difficult to defend a digital landscape is by customizing their malware.

Many organizations and individuals continue to use old, ineffective anti-malware software. If this software relies only on identifying signatures (distinguishing features of a threat), all the attackers have to do to evade it is to customize the malware. This can now be done very simply with no programming knowledge at all, using pre-packaged **software programs** that customize or adjust the malware to make its signature sufficiently different from those that anti-malware typically recognizes. This prevents the attack from being detected immediately, since an updated defense will not be added to a signature based anti-malware program until after the new malware version is discovered, isolated, submitted to anti-malware experts, decrypted, and analyzed. Depending on how exotic (unusual and rare) the customized malware is, creating a new defense against it may take months or years - and due to the sheer volume of new malware (estimated at over half a million new variants every day), it may not be feasible to update older forms of anti-malware quickly enough for them to provide a viable defense.

Added to this problem is the fact that a lot of malicious software is capable of adapting after installation to more effectively evade anti-malware. This form of anti-malware is known as ***polymorphic malware***.

Some of the more recent nextgen anti-malware does not have this deficit and can detect and block over 99% of these more sophisticated malware threats. However, as of early 2017, many enterprises are using anti-malware that misses more malware than it detects and deals with.

***polymorphic malware*** *- malicious software that can change its attributes to help avoid detection by* ***anti-malware****. This mutation process can be automated so that the function of the software continues, but the method of operation, location and other attributes may change. See also* ***metamorphic malware****.*

Password attacks

Far too much access to different computer systems and online services is controlled only by a username and password combination. Added to this, almost every service requires its own username and password. This has led most computer users to need tens and sometimes hundreds of different usernames and passwords.

However, instead of using different passwords and usernames for each online account, many people follow the unsafe practice of re-using the same ones.

In addition, security breaches at major online sites, including LinkedIn, Yahoo and others have made billions of username and password combinations openly available on the black market.

This has meant that instead of cracking passwords, criminals can easily process long lists of historic usernames and passwords into automated software that can check if they work in thousands of different online services.

If this was not bad enough, the criminal fraternity has also worked out ways of using statistics to bypass many of the password security measures used to block password 'guesses.' If they make more than a few attempts to guess a password at one site, the attempts may be blocked. However, if they work from multiple locations and make fewer attempts while distributing their guesses across thousands of services, the attempts are nearly impossible to detect.

This has led most major online services to add more layers to their access security. You may notice that this may take the form of a requirement to re-enter a password and a unique code that appears on the screen, or you may be required to receive a text message or email that provides a code that must be entered to confirm that the person logging in really is the account holder.

Some organizations used to blame account users for thefts of money or information that resulted from the use of a valid username and password, but investigations have proved that this is no longer a valid defense. For instance, a distributed robotic password attack using botnets can try thousands of passwords from thousands of locations on thousands of different attacks that will be undetectable through normal means. The majority of attempts will fail - but enough will be successful to make that approach worthwhile for the attacker.

The reality is that access to systems requires more than just a username and password to validate that whomever is asking for access really is the valid user.

Security experts have also discovered that many of the techniques that were previously recommended to strengthen passwords have the opposite effect. For example, using a chain of 4 or 5 random words in lower case letters is thousands of times more difficult to crack than a password with 8 characters that contains combinations of numbers, special characters, and upper and lower case letters.

These types of 8-character passwords are fairly easy to crack because password-cracking software is educated about human password patterns. For example, password guessing software can start by expecting that the first character is a capital letter and the last character is most likely to be a special character or set of numbers.

## DDoS (Distributed Denial of Service)

The distributed denial of service technique for interrupting a network connection or online service by sending in a large volume of unwanted traffic has been used for many years. However, what has recently changed is that launching a DDoS is now easy to do, and the amount of disruptive traffic that can be sent has vastly increased.

This is because computers and smartphones used to be practically the only Internet-connected devices, and now there are billions of other low-cost devices hooked up to the Internet. Most of these devices contain weak security, so it is easy for criminals to infect them with malware. In early 2017, it was estimated that some 80% of 'smart' devices actually have weak and vulnerable security.

It is now relatively easy for a cyber attacker to recruit tens of thousands of these weakly-protected devices and then use them to mount huge DDoS attacks, on a scale that would not have been considered possible a few years ago.

Other Evolving Attack Methods

A further significant but often overlooked area of compromise is the presence of ***USB*** connection ports on most hardware devices.

Many forms of data loss prevention security programs and hardware configuration seek to disable or limit access to these ports; however, hardware with malicious content is usually built to circumvent security measures. For example, USB connections may be limited to keyboards and mice, but a piece of malicious hardware may be programmed to resemble a keyboard or mouse. It may physically look like a mouse, but in addition to that function, it may also contain malware or memory to help with an attack.

A direct physical connection (for example via a USB connection) to a device that already has access inside a network will already be positioned beyond several layers of security, as it can leverage the existing access permissions of the device it was connected to.

This type of attack does require physical access to a device, but this can be achieved by a rogue insider who deliberately connects an infected USB device to a networked computer, or by a targeted employee or supplier who unintentionally uses an infected device given to him or her by a surreptitious attacker.

Statistics about the prevalence of malware-infected USB devices vary according to the samples used by different researchers, but studies do indicate that a significant minority of all USB devices carry malware.

Whenever you look at a cybersecurity statistic, it is always worth verifying its validity. How recent is it? Is the person or party delivering the message trying to sell something (could it be bias?)

Much of the cybercrime experienced leverages what is referred to as the ***dark web***.

***dark web** - websites that hide their server locations. Although publicly accessible, they are not registered on standard search engines, and the hidden server values make it extremely difficult to determine which organizations and people are behind these sites.*

Dark web locations are used for all kinds of illegal activities. When new vulnerabilities in software are announced, the exploit kit to take advantage of the problem is usually available over the dark web within 24 hours. The dark web is also used to sell stolen data, pay for disruption to services (DDoS attack as a service) and exchange other illegal forms of information. Criminals who use the dark web also use various encryption and privacy software tools to help hide their user details.

A final emerging attack trend that deserves consideration is the extent and continuing growth of mobile computing. Over half of all Internet traffic is already processed using some form of mobile device. The continuing increase in mobile and other Internet-connected devices other than traditional computers or laptops makes these devices increasingly popular targets for cyber criminals.

## Evolving Defense Methods

Given the scale and sophistication of attacks, it may seem to be nearly impossible to create effective defenses. However, this is not true.

As attacks become more sophisticated, defenses too are being strengthened. The main change that is occurring is that defense strategies are now being increasingly combined and placed in more locations.

For example, the increased usage of mobile devices has meant that a security technology known as ***mobile device management*** has become standard in large enterprises to manage the tablet and smart phone assets used by employees.

***Mobile Device Management (MDM)** - a technology used to securely control the operation and use of mobile **devices** such as tablets and smartphones. Able (for example) to remotely wipe information from a mobile device and control which **applications** and functions are permitted to be installed or run.*

As already discussed, using a password alone is no longer considered an adequate access control for any secure device. ***Multi-factor authentication*** is becoming a required standard rather than a high security option.

***multi-factor authentication*** *- using more than one form of proof to confirm the identity of a person or* ***device*** *attempting to request access. There are usually three different categories of* ***authentication*** *types: (i) something you know [often a password] (ii) something you have [perhaps a security token or access card] and (iii) something you are [the use of* ***biometrics;*** *for example fingerprint or facial recognition]. As an example, effective* ***two-factor authentication*** *would require that when access is being requested, proof would be required from at least two different categories.*

Perhaps the most significant improvement in security technologies is the use of something called machine learning to help detect and defeat attacks. Instead of having to specifically identify and block a known threat, many technologies, including the latest forms of anti-malware (often referred to as *nextgen* anti-malware and some types of advanced endpoint protection), are able to intelligently recognize and neutralize threats based purely on how each file and service is operating.

Whereas people formerly had to manually instruct security technologies how to recognize and neutralize a threat, machine learning programs can understand a computer system's regular and permitted behaviors so they are able to intelligently learn about, report and block suspicious items or events.

There are also technical traps that can be set to help capture, trace and prosecute attackers. ***Honeypots*** and ***honey networks*** are two examples of techniques cybersecurity professionals use that involve setting up fake digital areas that look like sensitive and valuable parts of an attack surface, but contain nothing of value. In fact, these traps are intentionally used to lure, identify and trace would-be attackers and their malware.

***honeypot*** *- an electronic* ***device*** *or collection of* ***data*** *that is designed to trap would-be* ***attackers*** *by detecting, deflecting or otherwise counteracting their efforts. Designed to look like a real part of an enterprise's* ***attack surface,*** *the honeypot will contain nothing of real value to the attacker, but will contain tools to identify, isolate and trace any intrusion.*

***honey network*** *- the collective name for a cluster of* ***honeypots*** *that operate to-*

*gether to help form part of a **network** intrusion detection strategy.*

Network recording is another newer tool being used by many large organizations. This allows weeks or months of network transactions to be replayed to help trace and identify the nature of an attack, even after it has ended.

There are also a number of non-technical strategies that can significantly diminish the potential for attack.

One such strategy involves data retention and destruction. Although collecting large amounts of information can sometimes be advantageous, individuals and organizations often keep a lot of information that is of limited or low value active in their networks. This is mostly because of the low cost of data storage and the perception that keeping the information is wiser than discarding it. However, keeping it is often detrimental.

Implementing well-thought-out data retention and destruction policies that consider the cost of security as part of an overall business strategy can help ensure that data is only kept active and available when keeping it is justifiable.

Email is a great example of this principle. When lawyers approach a case, it is easier to find single communications that indicate wrongdoing than it is to reassemble the full structured set of data that proves otherwise. If employees and other email system users understand that their communications are automatically deleted after, for example, 3 months, unless specifically stored to an archive system, then the risk exposure is lower.

Similarly, even if there are legal or business requirements to keep information stored, it is important to determine whether live, active storage is necessary or offline storage is satisfactory.

These measures help reduce the attack surface and focus security efforts.

If you consider the email theft from Mossack Fonseca, although they had out-of-date software and poor security configurations, the success of the attack largely derived from the fact that they had chosen to leave years and years of email in place online.

Another method of reducing an attack surface is to create high-security zones that add substantially more protection to the most sensitive data. Just as policies may govern the configuration of a high-security site, it is possible to mandate whether a high-security zone should be a ***closed system***, or whether all inbound and outbound traffic must be fully decrypted and inspected.

***closed system*** *– a collection of* ***applications, systems*** *and* ***devices*** *that only have the ability to communicate with each other. No connection to any component outside the known and trusted group is permitted.*

Closed systems are frequently used, for example, in manufacturing lines and aircraft control.

Most significantly, *all* technologies managing or connected to information or services of value have to have security embedded by design. Deploying security only on a network misses more than half of the potential vulnerabilities.

Even for the configuration of cloud services, or the use of supplier systems – any technology connected or used has to ensure that appropriate security requirements and testing are included from their earliest design stage through to their eventual retirement.

To summarize, it is possible to create highly effective defenses against attacks.

- The most critical factor in implementing such defenses in organizations is having executive (board-level) support for the correct investment into security. This requires presenting the executive with a clear picture of the size and scale of the organization's risk exposure. This is covered in greater detail in Chapters 12 & 13.
- Reduce the attack surface to the minimum appropriate size to meet the company's business needs.
- Use a security architect to help simplify the range of cyber defense points.
- Classify information to identify which sets of data require the greatest amount of security control.
- Zone the attack surface into discrete segments that reflect the value and sensitivity of the information they transact. Apply the greatest security to the highest-value zones.
- Remove or destroy data that has insignificant or low value.
- Use up-to-date 'nextgen' anti-malware across all devices that carry, store or transact your information.
- Ensure that you have strong user access controls that work on the basis of providing people with the lowest amount of privilege they require to perform their role.

- Ensure access controls require more than just a username and password to authenticate the identity of a user.
- Patch all devices and operating systems promptly with the latest security updates from their manufacturers.
- Deploy other key technical countermeasures such as advanced firewalls with strong policies to critical locations.
- Make sure the security settings on all applications, systems and physical devices are set to an appropriately high level and remove all default accounts.
- Educate your users on good security practices, including password management and how to recognize suspicious emails and attachments.
- Ensure all technologies that are built or configured for use have security requirements included and tested throughout their lifecycle.

Remember that defense in depth requires a holistic view of security. Physical security, procedural controls and cultural conditions are key contributors to the most significant and successful attacks.

Only organizations with an informed view of the full picture will be able to prevent substantial attacks.

The primary challenge to creating an effective organizational defense is securing sufficient investment in the necessary technologies and measures. Procuring this investment requires building an effective business case (justification for the expense). With the number of successful attacks that result in enormous losses making headlines, the value of improved security over electronic devices and their data will be relatively easy to demonstrate.

Effective security over electronic devices and their information requires an expensive and extensive approach that is championed at the board level.

Ineffective security is even more expensive. Under-investment in security is in fact now frequently leading to the dismissal of key board members who were poorly informed about the cyber risks they were allowing their organization to take.

# 10. Case Study – Sony (2014)

| | |
|---|---|
| Organization(s): | Sony |
| Breach Dates: | Unknown to unknown |
| Date of Discovery: | 24th November 2014 |
| Date of Disclosure: | 24th November 2014 |
| Nature of the Breach: | Sensitive emails, unreleased films, employee data, .... |
| Scale of the Breach: | Believed to be in excess of 100 terabytes. |
| Impact: | Estimated > $300m |

<u>Summary:</u>

As a very large company, highly reliant on technology, Sony had frequently been the target of cyber attacks in the past.

To provide flexibility for their diverse divisions, Sony operated a flexible approach to the security of their systems, allowing each group of companies to implement and manage what each required, at the same time as having some overall security systems that operated across all divisions.

This approach has the advantage of allowing different divisions to incorporate new technologies to help expand and deliver products to fulfill customer needs and in turn to increase revenues.

This strategy can work well, but entails much higher operating costs than top-down security enforcement does. When running security separately for each division, it is vital to understand what the responsibilities and boundaries are for each section. Adequate funding must be in place, and it must be sufficient to allow each division to manage a comprehensive approach to security, including all the components we have explored in this book.

On Friday 21st November 2014, a small number of Sony's executive email accounts received a communication from a group calling itself 'God'sApstls,' demanding monetary compensation to prevent Sony from 'being bombarded as a whole.' The recipients reportedly ignored or treated this communication as spam.

On Monday 24th November 2014, Sony Pictures Entertainment, a division of the Sony Corporation, discovered that a significant number of their systems had been compromised. A substantial amount of data had already been taken, and a number of critical services were rendered inoperable. The exact causes and infiltration points were unknown at this point.

The first reports of the attack being detected surfaced when employee computer screens at Sony Pictures Entertainment headquarters in Culver City, California, began flashing with a message from the hackers. The message included links to some of the stolen data the hackers had collected. At this time the attackers identified themselves as the 'Guardians of Peace.'

That same day, information about the breach spread quickly through social media. Some of the stolen data had been posted online, and the media began to examine the contents.

The extent of the attack and the time it took to identify the method of attack had a significant impact on Sony's immediate operations. Indeed, Sony employees around the world allegedly continued to work without being able to use their computers, email or voicemail for many days.

Over the following weeks, more and more stolen data was posted online, along with threats and demands from the attackers.

The extent of the breach was enormous. Data posted online included:

- Entire email archives from senior executives.
- Information on some employees, including payroll information and social security numbers.
- Unreleased films.
- Company financial information.
- ...

The entire list of the types of information the attackers exposed would fill several pages. The attackers (the Guardians of Peace) initially (that same month) revealed that they had managed to take over 12 terabytes of information.

Indications are that the malware the hackers used continued working for some time, even after the attack was detected. Final assessments put the amount of data the hackers removed at over 100 terabytes. To put that figure in perspective, the entire US Library of Congress in digital format is just 10% of that size.

This ongoing exfiltration of information indicated that the malware was polymorphic (as outlined in the previous chapter), and, at the time, could not be blocked or quarantined with existing anti-malware. So even though Sony's security team attempted to quarantine or remove the stolen data, these attempts were unsuccessful.

Other security measures that were in place, such as firewalls that should have closed down the system in an emergency, also failed to immediately block or prevent the ongoing outflow of information. This indicated that the malware was bypassing these defenses as well as evading the anti-malware software.

The sensitivity level of the information being stolen was mixed, with benign (relatively insignificant) data frequently existing alongside small pockets of highly sensitive information.

Indications were that the attack was politically motivated by the upcoming release of a film called *The Interview*, which reportedly offended the North Korean government.

Sony engaged external security companies to assist with efforts to block and remove the exposed data and to help restore internal systems and services. The magnitude of the attack also led US government agencies to assist.

On the 19th December, the US Computer Emergency Response Team posted information about a new type of destructive malware that had recently been used to attack a major media company.

https://www.us-cert.gov/ncas/alerts/TA14-353A

Analysis of the malware confirmed that it was capable of listening to, accessing, commanding and destroying information on the devices it infected. Analysts described this malware as a **worm**.

***worm** – a form of malicious software (**malware**) that seeks to find other locations to which it can replicate. This helps to both protect the malware from removal and to increase the area of the **attack surface** that is compromised.*

It worked by leveraging a standard file sharing protocol called a **s**ever **m**essage **b**lock, or SMB. Because the worm could also delete information, it was also referred to as a 'wiper.' This approach had been used in other attacks, and a number of patches were available that could have helped address this vulnerability.

The financial impact, including loss of revenues, disruption to operations, costs for remediation and compensation payments are still ongoing at the time this book is being written. These costs are expected to total several hundreds of millions of dollars, if not more.

The scale, magnitude and impact of this attack completely outstripped the cybersecurity capabilities that Sony had in place.

<u>Root Cause Analysis:</u>

The Sony cybersecurity team had never adequately considered or prepared for a breach of this magnitude that might affect Sony itself or the Sony Pictures Entertainment division.

When Sony Pictures produced a film that offended an insulated, sensitive and reactionary nation state, Sony added a substantial and powerful adversary to the list of attackers who would be interested in infiltrating its systems.

Unlike other attacks, in which the motive would usually be money-related, a state-sponsored attack often includes very different objectives.

The foundation of an adequate cybersecurity defense-in-depth strategy relies on informing a company's executives about the extent of the risks and ensuring that a holistic understanding of the level of exposure exists.

Based on the extent of the infiltration and the resulting damage, it is evident that a key root cause was the large number of gaps in the defense layers. Overall, the amount of data that was taken indicates that data loss prevention tools at network and device levels were either bypassed or absent; either way, these tools proved to be ineffective.

Although it was (at that time) nearly impossible to fully protect a system against an attack that uses polymorphic malware, the malware itself mostly leverages known exploits for which protective measures already existed. This means that although an attack using polymorphic malware can create damage, the scale and impact can be substantially reduced when all other security measures are operating effectively.

As we covered in the last chapter, putting hardened, defense in depth in place is expensive, and so is regularly updating cyber defenses based on evolving methods of attack. But this type of breach reveals the fact that not investing in holistic, frequently-updated defenses can end up costing more than strong, adaptable defense in depth does.

Although speculation has continued about whether or not the Sony breach was actually instigated by North Korea, a few key facts indicate this to be the case.

The type of software used to infiltrate Sony, though modified to help it evade anti-malware, was very similar to that used in an earlier attack made on South Korea in March 2013. That attack was also attributed to North Korea.

In addition, having infiltrated and copied unreleased films from Sony, the 'Guardians of Peace' posted those films online, except for 'The Interview,' – the one that offended the North Korean government.

The initial infiltration was tracked back to the St. Regis Bangkok hotel in Thailand.

Analysts also found evidence that the malware may have been present and remained undetected within Sony's systems for some time prior to the date that the attack was revealed. This evidence supported the observation that it would have been very difficult to collect and steal the amount of data that was involved in a time span of less than several months.

The malware used exploits (specific techniques) that were known for some time, and had Sony installed patches (updates) that were available from software manufacturers, their systems would have resisted the 'known' exploits.

Once the attack was known to be in progress, it appeared that the company was unable to rapidly update their intrusion detection and prevention routines to block the attack. This provides further support for the argument that the failure to routinely install updates played a big role in increasing Sony's vulnerability to an attack of this magnitude.

Analysts also found that Sony's record retention and destruction procedures, at least for email systems, were either nonexistent or highly deficient. Automatically removing and destroying email after a specific, limited time period, unless it was explicitly earmarked for retention, would have substantially reduced the impact of the data exposure.

In other words, the size and sensitivity of the attack surface was larger and more vulnerable than it needed to be because of deficiencies in patch management and records retention and destruction policies.

Additionally, the attackers were able to locate some sensitive data alongside non-sensitive data. This indicated that information classification processes were not fully in place. Sensitive information was not consistently separated and subject to higher security measures than non-sensitive data was.

There has been unsubstantiated speculation that another root cause of the attack involved disaffected former employees leveraging inside information. Part of the rationale for this accusation is that the extent of the damage and infiltration could be more rationally explained if the attackers had a reasonable understanding of Sony systems, network locations and vulnerability points to assist them in planning their attack strategy.

A final root cause of the breach is that one of the key features of all good security is single point accountability.

**single point (of) accountability** *(SPA or SPOA) – the principle that all critical* **assets,** *processes and actions must have clear ownership and traceability to a single person. The rationale is that the absence of a defined, single owner is a frequent cause of process or asset protection failure. Shared ownership is regarded as a significant security gap due to the consistent demonstration that security flaws have an increased probability of persisting when more than one person is accountable.*

At the beginning of this book I presented the statement, 'Nobody ever made a statue to honor a committee. Operating a divisional approach to security can work, but requires clear and accountable lines of single point accountability to be defined. If everyone is responsible, often nobody is accountable. Who was the person ultimately responsible for Sony's security? Was it the executive at the division level, or the executive at the corporate level?

These types of poorly-defined accountability policies lead to slow and inadequate responses in the face of agile and fast-moving attackers. Each organization must adopt a security posture that reflects the value of its information and the types of attackers they are likely to encounter.

In summary, Sony did not have the scale of defense-in-depth security controls in place to manage the threat that materialized. They did not sufficiently anticipate or prepare for an attack that could potentially impact them on this scale.

# 11. The Cybersecurity Cold War

There is a war going on right now. Each day, hundreds of millions of attempts are made to gain unauthorized access into digital devices and accounts. This has been particularly highlighted by the hacking incidents and the exposure of stolen emails that were allegedly perpetrated to influence the 2016 US Presidential election.

Some cyber attacks are opportunistic, and some are targeted, but all of them are motivated by the desire to create political or financial gain over the organizations and individuals that rightfully own these assets.

The increase in the number of attempts and the cost of the consequences is both a cause of great concern and a strong motivating factor in the drive to improve cybersecurity and cyber defenses.

As with any war, strategists need to know their enemy. Who are the organizations and people that want to target diverse digital landscapes, what are their goals, how sophisticated are they and how do they operate?

Cyber attackers (also sometimes called ***threat actors***) mainly fall into 8 groups:

1. Nation States
2. Terrorist Groups
3. Organized Criminal Groups
4. ***Hacktivist*** Communities (***Hacktivism***)
5. Skilled Professional Hackers
6. Disaffected or Opportunistic Insiders
7. Amateur Hackers & Journalists
8. Anyone

Every organization's ***threatscape*** is different. Based on what you or your organization does, you can become a more or less attractive target for one or more of these groups.

***hacktivism*** *– an amalgamation of* ***hacker*** *and activism. Describes the act of seeking* ***unauthorized access*** *into any* ***digital device*** *or* ***digital landscape*** *to promote a social or political agenda. Usually the unauthorized access is used to cause destruction, disruption and/or publicity. Individuals participating in these acts are* *called* ***hacktivists.***

***hacktivist*** *– an amalgamation of the words* ***hacker*** *and activist. Describes any individual who participates in* ***hacktivism.***

***threatscape*** *– a term that amalgamates* ***threat*** *and land****scape****. An umbrella term to describe the overall, expected methods (****vectors****) and types of* ***cyber attackers*** *through or by which an organization or individual might expect to be attacked.*

The size, scale and public profile of your digital presence will also be a key factor in determining who attacks you and how often.

In 2017, most household cybersecurity continues to be very poor. This will change quickly.

The level of effort and sophistication required for a cyber attacker to profit from any cyber attack is quickly decreasing. As the required effort diminishes, more and more households are prone to attack and become aware of the need to invest in greater and greater levels of cybersecurity.

The attraction of attacking private households will also increase with the growing trend of connecting more and more everyday household and other general electronics to each other. This is known as the ***Internet of Things***.

***Internet of Things* (IoT)*** *– the incorporation of electronics into everyday items sufficient to allow them to* ***network*** *(communicate) with other network-capable* ***devices.***

One of the primary issues with successful cyber attacks is that unlike a physical battle, the attacker does not need to be of significant size or sophistication to inflict a great deal of damage. Even when the group behind an attack is large and organized, the number of people required for a devastating attack can be as low as one.

The cost to reward ratio for any cyber criminal is so high that many of the groups are investing heavily in increasing their inventory of skills and tools to leverage other peoples' dependence on technology for their own gain.

An additional significant factor is that it has become easy for anyone with relatively little knowledge to download and use tools for cyber attacks. Hackers no longer need to have programming skills; they can simply use these ready-made tools that are widely available and often cost nothing.

We will now look more closely at each of the groups that conduct cyber attacks to better understand their motives and targets.

### Nation States

Countries have engaged in espionage throughout history. Modern technologies have moved espionage to a new level.

The former German Democratic Republic (GDR or East Germany) possibly had the most well-developed internal espionage network of any country in history. Official statistics indicate that their secret police, called the 'Stasi,' had approximately 1 in every 20 adult citizens as either employees or informants. I spoke with a former Stasi informant. He believes the figure was in fact much higher than 1 in 20; possibly as high as 1 in 5.

Before digital technologies were available, monitoring the activities of large numbers of people involved a huge amount of effort and very large financial investments. In the case of the Stasi, estimates place the number of people on the payroll at around 274,000.

Modern technologies allow similar activities to be managed at a much lower cost. Large numbers of people are no longer needed to monitor others' communications. Technologies can be programmed to 'spy' on all spoken or written communications and to raise a flag or alert whenever particular words or phrases are used, or when particular people communicate.

Large-scale monitoring focuses mainly on intelligence gathering. The more significant current threat from sovereign states is the potential for them to more completely infiltrate and leverage other countries' critical information or infrastructure.

The motivations for nation state-sponsored cyber attacks can be summarized as follows:

- The acquisition of intelligence to prevent attacks and to exert influence.
- The theft of intellectual property to understand enemy capabilities and leverage the information towards domestic political or financial gains.

- The ability to exert control over any foreign or domestic enemy through their digital landscape. For example, by having the ability to remotely disable critical enemy technologies and services.

An example of the last motivation on the list occurred during the 2016 US Presidential election campaign, when the US had first-hand experience with the use of stolen information to exert influence over the election's outcome.

According to sources in the US security community, the nation states with the highest cyber warfare capabilities are:

1.) United States & China are both in first place.

    China has enormous cyber intelligence and penetration capabilities. These capabilities tend to be used passively to gather information and steal intellectual property. China does not tend to practice destructive techniques; however, this makes it more difficult to detect its intrusions and contributes to the fact that its capacity to create sudden and immense damage through cyber infiltration is much greater than that of any other country.

    The United States also has considerable infiltration capabilities, and on the flip side bears the distinction of being the most cyber-attacked country on the planet. As a result, the US has developed what are probably the best defensive cyber strategies in the world.

    As an example of American cyberwar aptitude, in early 2015, security analysts identified a new type of malware used by a group of hackers known as 'The Equation,' (the group is alleged to be linked to the US National Security Agency). This malware penetrates the low-level programming found in many major hard disk brands. The approach is so advanced that at the time, traditional anti-malware and even fully re-formatting the drives could not remove it. However, the malware has only been found in the digital systems of specific institutions that are associated with US government interests.

3) Russia

    Russia has increased its focus on cyber intelligence in recent years. Unlike those used by China, Russian infiltration techniques allegedly do tend to be intentionally more noticeable. These techniques are easier to identify but more expensive to correct. Russia is also a leading exponent of 'hybrid warfare,' in which cyber attacks are combined with other subversive techniques to increase Russia's power and territorial advantages at the expense of other nations' safety and security. The US 2016 election campaign was not the first or last time Russia has allegedly used this tactic. One aspect of Russia's standard strategies includes creating enough doubt and confusion about any 'information' that the validity of everything is called into question. This is often achieved by calling legitimate information fake and fake information 'fake news.' The subsequent public confusion can both create and leverage bias in governments and citizens alike in order to achieve the perpetrators' political goals.

4) Israel, the UK and France are positioned in equal fourth place.

North Korea is also worthy of mention. Although it has very limited Internet access, the government has realized how much power and influence it can exert through effective cyber infiltration techniques. The Sony cybersecurity breach in late 2014 is a great example of this.

It is difficult to obtain reliable information on the scale of state-sponsored cyber warfare. For obvious reasons, both attacking and defending states do not want to reveal what they do or what they know.

What is clear is that countries worldwide are spending a lot of time and money to step up both their defensive and offensive capabilities.

There is also a growing amount of cooperation between allied states to share information about new and emerging threats.

Governments do not only focus their efforts on other countries; they also infiltrate significant organizations that can be useful to them. Google, Microsoft, Apple, humanitarian organizations, infrastructure services, and even major banks must defend their systems from intrusion by some nation states.

Many nation state 'employees' are not averse to making money on the side as a peripheral benefit from their cyber sleuthing activities. These individuals may find information that is not useful to the state for which they work, but if they can earn money from it on another market, they may well do it.

**Terrorist Groups**

Terrorist groups have three main motives when it comes to cyber attacks:

1) To raise funds.
2) To create a negative impact on their enemies.

3) To raise their profile.

One of the attractions that cyber attacks have for these groups is that these attacks can potentially cause a great deal of damage, using relatively small numbers of resources. A terrorist group only has to identify a single cyber weakness to be successful. Conversely, their enemies must sustain cyber defenses across a much wider territory.

Although some terrorists may attempt to portray themselves as hacktivism groups, there is a key behavioral difference. Terrorist groups, although they may have political goals, use organized, illegal, destructive methods to achieve their goals. Running scams to defraud people and other institutions to achieve financial gain is a major source of revenue for some of these groups.

### Organized Criminal Groups

The motivation behind any organized criminal group is very clear. Money.

This financial gain can be realized directly or indirectly. Stealing and re-using credit card information, or accessing a banking system and moving funds, are examples of direct methods used for financial gain. Acquiring information that allows blackmail or other forms of extortion to be used is an example of an indirect, but still effective, method of achieving financial gain.

Other hackers also use these methods, but there is a key difference between the cyber attack and extortion techniques used by individual hackers and those used by organized criminal groups:

Organized criminal groups have the structure, scale and funding to be able to mount stronger attacks and to make better, faster use of any information they acquire. If a lone hacker acquires millions of passwords, that person may try to sell the information on the dark web, but that process will reveal the problem to others (including law enforcement), alert the affected parties and reduce the damages to the victims and the financial gain to the attacker. An organized criminal group can better monetize the data without openly revealing they have it. This means they can potentially make more money from it.

### Hacktivism

There is a fine line between hacktivism and terrorism. Both have political goals. The three main factors that generally characterize hacktivist groups are:

- The people involved believe they are serving a greater good. Examples are save the planet or remove corrupt government officials.
- The individuals involved do not seek to raise funds from their activities.
- Hacktivist groups will not intentionally engage in crimes that directly harm people or affect peoples' personal finances.

Any group that does not stay within these boundaries is a terrorist group.

Despite these boundaries, hacktivists still engage in criminal behavior. Specifically, they still aim to gain unauthorized access or cause damage to other organizations' digital landscapes.

The nature of the work that a particular enterprise or organization does usually influences the likelihood that it will be targeted by hacktivist groups.

### Skilled Professional Hackers

These are the assassins for hire of the cyber attack world. A distinction needs to be drawn between professional ethical hackers and professional criminal hackers.

Ethical hackers, (also known as 'white hats'), are paid by the customer to reveal gaps and weaknesses in the customer's defenses.

Unlike ethical hackers, who only use their skills to expose (but not leverage) technical gaps in cyber defenses, skilled professional criminal hackers ('black hats') have monetary goals without ethical standards. Professional criminal hackers use their talents for monetary gain without regard for the law.

Professional hackers are extremely up to date with the latest technologies and exploits. Just like any cybersecurity expert, a professional hacker may solely focus on technical intrusions or can use diverse skills such as social engineering or other attack techniques in combination with his or her technical ability.

Independent professional hackers with diverse skills are more dangerous than those who rely solely on technical measures. Independent professional hackers engaged by organizations to 'red team' an environment will usually walk away knowing how to bring that organization down.

### Disaffected or Opportunistic Insiders

People with access to systems inside any organization or supplier have permitted access that already takes them past many layers of defense.

Enterprises with very strong cybersecurity defenses can reduce the possibility of misuse by rogue, criminal or otherwise disaffected insiders to a very low level by always monitoring and supervising privileged access. When these controls are in place, it usually takes a collaborative effort to create substantial impact.

However, sometimes an insider who gains access to even a comparatively small amount of information - for example, a single email - can use it to create substantial damage.

As covered in the chapter on Human Factors, pre-employment screening and ongoing monitoring and assessment can help detect potential rogue insiders, but these are not foolproof methods.

A disaffected individual is usually motivated by the amount of damage he or she can cause to the person or enterprise by which they feel aggrieved.

An opportunistic insider, on the other hand, is more likely to stumble into a situation in which he or she believes it is possible to achieve financial gains without being detected or losing his or her position.

As an example, a pharmaceutical company (not one for which I have worked) discovered a new drug formula that showed a lot of promise. When the company tried to patent the formula, the patent office discovered the drug was already being produced and sold in China. Investigators learned that a trusted employee in China had stolen a copy of the formula and sold it for just a few thousand dollars. Despite this fact, the drug could no longer be patented. The thief went to prison for a very long time, but the pharmaceutical company lost potential revenues in the hundreds of millions of dollars.

The main defense against this type of attack is to foster a strong, supportive and positive security culture within an enterprise and to provide employees and suppliers with examples of the consequences of these types of behavior. It is also necessary to ensure that any sensitive information is only accessible or removable with appropriate safeguards.

Audit trails, access permissions, data loss prevention, email screening tools, random physical searches, supervision, and restrictions on the use of cameras in the workplace are all examples of security controls that can be used to deter or prevent this type of behavior.

An enterprise with a culture that makes employees and suppliers feel remote and unengaged is likely to create disaffected people with insider access.

In a similar manner, an enterprise that does not tightly secure sensitive information that can be subverted for financial gain is also likely to suffer from cybersecurity breaches perpetrated by opportunistic insiders.

A major concern with this type of threat is that the insider does not necessarily need to possess any cyber attack skills at all to be successful.

### Amateur Hackers and Journalists

A nation state that I will not name here created a very sophisticated, effective hacking tool that cost millions of dollars to develop. The state then made it freely available for download on the Internet.

Why? Easy answer – the state could defend itself against the tool, and it also allowed this state to upload its own malware to other hackers and to identify who these hackers were. The state derived large amounts of new intelligence through the activities of the hackers who used the software.

This is one way in which even the most amateur hacker or journalist after a story can obtain very sophisticated but totally free, hacking tools.

One danger posed by amateur hackers is that they will not necessarily be deterred by defenses that will prevent professionals from striking. If a professional hacker encounters a defense that is likely to lead him or her to be caught if he or she compromises it, this hacker will probably leave it alone. Although the actions of an amateur are relatively easy to trace, his or her exploits can still create substantial damage in unexpected places.

Amateurs are also more likely to target practically anything, without any understanding of the target's value or consequences. Journalists may use a more targeted approach because their motivation is to obtain newsworthy information.

### Anyone

The ease of launching cyber attacks means that practically anyone can be a perpetrator. Organizations that study cyber attacks and their consequences believe three major changes have led to this reality:

1) To be successful at a cybersecurity attack previously required a lot of expertise and specialized tools that were difficult to obtain. Nowadays, anyone can attempt an attack using software (packed with malware of its own) that can be downloaded, often for free, over the Internet.

2) The cost and potential value that can be extracted from a successful cyber attack have increased exponentially.
3) Cryptocurrencies (such as Bitcoin) are forms of online payment that can hide the identity of the recipient. If used carefully, they can help anybody achieve an anonymous payment method for ransoms or other forms of extortion or revenue.

Although most high-damage cybersecurity breaches are perpetrated by skilled or organized groups, it is easy for any individual with a personal motive to engage in this type of criminal activity.

Back in 2015, it was relatively rare for private individuals to try to steal information or penetrate the defenses of organizations or households. Now, the proliferation of free tools means that this form of attack is increasing, especially as attacks on from overseas are currently extremely difficult to police and prosecute.

The threatscape for each enterprise or individual is different. Depending on what an organization or individual does, different predatory groups and people may seek to take advantage of their digital landscape.

The number of attacks and level of automation with which they are carried out is immense. Do not underestimate the extent of the cyber war that is taking place.

The speed with which emerging technologies are being adopted and used means that our ability to use technology safely is always a few steps behind the latest threats. There are a lot of groups and individuals out there who are ready to take advantage of these vulnerabilities.

The mantra for any effective cybersecurity is to ensure that there is always a comprehensive, defense-in-depth strategy actively operating to protect a digital landscape. Individuals and organizations are more likely to survive each battle if multiple, effective layers of defense are in place... And those layers need to extend beyond the network perimeter to wherever the information of value flows.

Cybersecurity designs and plans should always include an understanding of the organizations and people that may attack a digital landscape, along with an understanding of how they operate and how to ensure that adequate protection is in place. This threat intelligence analysis is usually part of the overall cybersecurity risk assessment that any Chief Information Security Officer regularly performs.

# 12. Risk-Based Cybersecurity & Stacked Risk

What should be evident from all the case studies is that any organization that is caught out by substantial breaches in its cybersecurity lacked a clear understanding of the risks they were taking. These organizations self-evidently admitted that they lacked a connected and informed view of their active risks.

Effective cybersecurity management relies on accurate capture and escalation of priority risks. If significant issues or problems are not consistently captured at an individual level and appropriately escalated when necessary, the executive management team will operate in an uninformed environment, with no sense of the true gaps and their comparative priorities.

In this chapter we cover:

- What is a cybersecurity risk?
- How do you capture and manage individual risks?
- How do you deal with measuring, monitoring, and managing clusters of risks using:
    - Risk Registers
    - Risk Assessments
- How to apply ***risk-based*** cybersecurity management.

Managing risks individually, though important, will still create issues if an overview of the collective risks is not possible because of deficiencies in cybersecurity systems.

When organizations incur major financial losses as a result of intrusions and data losses, it is always the case that a chain of separate and unresolved risks existed. We will refer to this as ***stacked risks*** and will cover this topic in greater detail in the Cyber Risk Register section of this chapter.

> ***stacked risk*** *- the phenomenon of allowing seemingly separate potential issues with potential impact (**risks**) affecting the same **digital landscape** to accumulate. Without adequate identification and resolution, individual risks can form a toxic accumulation of issues that can be leveraged together to create a risk substantially greater than the individual components suggest. Megabreaches are usually the result of stacked risk in combination with a motivated **attacker**.*

Before we look at what risk is, it is useful to consider the general problems and prejudices that people have in their understanding of any type of risk.

Consider the following items and what comparative magnitude of threat to life you think they would pose, based on the number of deaths they cause annually in North America:

- Vending machines
- Brown bear attacks.
- Soft toys.
- Being left-handed.

Without any metrics or analysis, we can easily develop a distorted impression of the true dangers these things pose.

In fact, vending machines kill more people in North America each year (by falling on people when they rock them to recover loose items) than brown bears. Soft toys are responsible for more deaths than either brown bears or vending machines. Being left-handed is believed to cause the most deaths among these factors, through accidents caused by left-handed people using equipment designed for right-handed people.

(A much-debated study reported in 1991 by psychologists Diane Halpern and Stanley Coren showed a significant difference between life expectancy for left-handed and right-handed people. The study was later dismissed by many because it seemed to contain some statistical anomalies. However, based on other studies, social scientists and epidemiologists agree that left-handed people using equipment designed for right-handed people does cause a substantially greater number of accidents for them.)

- There were 11 deaths attributed to soft toys recorded in the US in 2012, according to the US Consumer Product Safety Commission.
- Two or three people die in the US each year due to vending machine accidents.
- An average of one person is killed in North America each year by brown bears.
- The number of fatalities due to being left-handed is unrecorded.

How is this relevant to cybersecurity?

The same issue emerges in cybersecurity; without an accurate understanding of the numbers that underlie certain risks, we can and do make mistakes about where to focus our security efforts and budget.

Without a full picture of the risks, as a cybersecurity manager, I might be tempted to prioritize spending on data encryption because it covers a significant amount of the potential attack surface. However, if I had full visibility of the issues and the comparative costs and benefits of certain countermeasures, I could easily determine that twenty or more higher-priority, higher-impact and lower-cost factors should be addressed first.

Since the largest unresolved risks create the most damage, it's important to have a comprehensive and connected view of the overall risks to be able to accurately understand where the cybersecurity priorities should be.

When risks are presented in isolation, it is not possible to understand their comparative priority.

Before we discuss the overall, comprehensive view, we still need to understand the basics of capturing and managing individual risks.

## What is a Cybersecurity Risk?

Anything that has the potential to cause detrimental impact to the electronic devices we use, or the information they store or transact, can be considered a cybersecurity risk. Remember, risks to the cyber environment can result from both technical and non-technical sources.

For example, if a problem exists with an organization failing to regularly provide security awareness training, this can still pose a cybersecurity risk because it has a significant potential to lead to poor usage practices by staff that in turn can facilitate an increased number of successful malware attacks.

Earlier in the book, we looked at threats, vulnerabilities and other gaps. Each of these factors can become a source of risk when it has (i) enough probability of occurring and (ii) the potential to cause significant detrimental impact if it does occur.

This is because the only 2 critical ingredients for a risk are:

1) Probability (also referred to as potential, likelihood or chance) of the problem occurring.
2) Impact of a sufficient magnitude to be of material concern.

There are a number of ways to measure probability. The most effective method is to ensure that all expressions of likelihood or the chances of something happening are translated into a percentage value. It is not possible or essential for the initial probability percentage assigned to a risk to be completely correct. That is because the percentage value assigned to each risk will become increasingly accurate as the information about the risk grows.

There are also many different ways to measure impact. The most effective way is to translate the cost of the potential disruption into a financial amount that reflects both (i) the cost to fix or restore the problem after it has occurred, and ii) the total cost to the organization that the problem can generate.

Remember, the cost to the organization due to disruption, loss of earnings or brand damage often contributes the highest amount to the financial impact estimate.

In both cases, without a numeric value, it is not possible to evaluate the risk in any meaningful way. That is because the people recording and monitoring risk would otherwise not be able to compare risks on a common scale.

For example, if I have a risk (**risk A**) that can create one million dollars worth of damage, and another risk (**risk B**) that can create ten million dollars worth of damage, they may both be considered to be 'very high' impact, depending on the size and budget of the organization. Only by having tangible numbers can I determine that one of those risks is ten times higher than the other and therefore more likely to be a higher priority to resolve.

Risk managers often use a simple mathematical formula to help identify priorities. By multiplying the probability (%) of the risk by the potential impact ($), I can arrive at an adjusted risk figure that can help me prioritize my risks.

- **Risk A** has a 75% chance of occurring and a one million dollar cost if it does occur.

  0.75 x 1,000,000 = $0.75m

- **Risk B** has a 5% chance of occurring and a ten million dollar cost if it does occur.

  0.05 x 10,000,000 = $0.5m

Although **risk B** has a higher potential financial impact, by incorporating the probability, we can determine that the higher likelihood of **risk A** occurring means we should seek to address **risk A** first.

However, there is also a third, critical parameter to consider: *proximity.*

Proximity is a measurement of time to help assess how soon we expect the risk to be active and problematic.

For example, we might be launching a new service in six month's time that is associated with **risk A**, but **risk B** could be a gap or problem that is already active. In that situation, we may reasonably choose to tackle the immediate risk sooner than the risk that is not yet an active problem.

Capturing basic numerical information about a risk is a key step towards managing it.

The basic ingredients for determining whether or not something is a risk are the presence of enough probability and impact to make the item significant enough to track. This is known as ***materiality***.

***materiality*** *– to have a level of significance or magnitude to be of concern.*

Generally, the larger the organization, the greater the financial impact must be before something is considered to have enough materiality to be recorded and managed as a risk.

If I have identified an individual, critical vulnerability in a single application, it is only likely to be considered a risk if it could (on its own) create substantial impact to my organization. I will still need to ensure it is managed to closure through normal processes, but I will not need to ask for it to be tracked as a risk.

However, I may also determine that the same critical vulnerability could be present in a large number of other applications and thus needs urgent investigation. In that case, I would escalate it as a risk if I thought the collective impact was significant.

Each organization defines its materiality threshold, usually as a financial amount. If a gap or problem has the potential to cause the organization more than $x of financial risk (where x is the materiality threshold determined by the organization), it should be captured into the risk management process.

There is more about materiality in the Risk Register section of this chapter.

## How Do You Capture and Manage Individual Risks?

When a risk is reported, it is important to then manage it effectively.

Managing individual risks effectively requires a consistent approach to the way in which each risk is captured and managed. Using consistent processes creates risk information that can more easily be compared, connected, escalated (if necessary) and prioritized later on.

There are several risk frameworks available, including ISO 31000 (the International Organization for Standardization's approach to Risk Management), COSO (from the **C**ommittee **o**f **S**ponsoring **O**rganizations of the Treadway Commission), the Enterprise Risk Management Framework and ISACA CRISC (Certification for Risks in Information Systems Control).

All of the above frameworks are worthy and can be explored further, depending on your personal or organizational preferences. For our purposes we will look at the core concepts that all risk frameworks share.

The 3 key ingredients are:

- Ownership: Ensure that each active risk has a clearly accountable owner.
- Lifecycle: Define and use a consistent risk lifecycle to ascertain what state the risk is in.
- Risk Information: Ensure that adequate information about the risk is captured, including its probability and impact.

### Ownership

Each individual risk must have a clearly assigned owner who accepts accountability for managing the risk. Single point accountability is just as important here as it is throughout the security framework. Other people can and will help to manage and control a risk, but there must be one specific person in control who is accountable for managing the risk through to eventual closure.

### Lifecycle

All individual risks have a lifecycle. They are discovered, investigated, analyzed, treated and closed as necessary. The simplest risk lifecycle may only consider a risk to be either 'open' (still a potential threat), or 'closed' (no longer a potential concern).

The more refined your risk lifecycle stages are, the easier it will be later on to differentiate new risks that are still being investigated from other risks that are further along the risk management process.

A useful basic set of lifecycle stages is:

- Identified
- Investigating
- Analyzing
- Treating
- Monitoring
- Closed

These do not need to be followed sequentially. For example, there will be some risks that are reported (identified), investigated, found to not be a risk, and closed.

Risk Information

In addition to a brief description of the risk, it is important to capture other key information about it. As covered in the previous section, it is essential to ensure that information about the probability and impact is captured. It does not matter if this is not accurate at first because the information about the risk should be increasingly clarified (or elaborated) during its lifecycle.

Risk information is more effective when it is captured in ways that make the risk's impact easier to analyze later on. For example, rather than recording impact information only in free text, it is more useful when multiple-choice lists can be leveraged. As shown below, this could allow the risk owner to select multiple factors or systems that could be impacted:

- Loss of critical service(s)
- Loss of critical product(s)
- Brand / organization image
- Customer data
- Company data
- Employee data
- Business processes
- Financial processes
- Internal applications
- External applications
- Regulatory or legal compliance

- Intellectual Property

Other standard risk information might include proximity (how soon the risk may occur) and manageability (how capable the risk owner believes the organization is of controlling the risk if it chooses to do so).

Generally, information about who reported a risk and when (date and time) this happened is also recorded.

Risk owners also (during analysis) determine which method or methods of risk management are appropriate. These methods are known as risk countermeasures or risk treatment options. There are normally up to 5 primary ways to deal with (treat) a risk:

- Prevention. This involves defeating the risk's cause and thereby preventing the risk from being present. For example, a risk manager may decide against adopting a particular technical component that is known to cause the risk. This is sometimes considered to be a form of avoiding the risk.
- Reduction. This involves doing less of something to diminish its potential impact. For example, reducing the number of records that a system stores can diminish its potential loss exposure.
- Acceptance. Accepting a risk means doing nothing, if its potential probability and impact are low enough to absorb and if pursuing other risk treatment methods is too expensive.
- Contingency. This means creating a fall-back plan to help decrease the impact from the risk if it does materialize. For example, having an alternative system or process that can take over if the system at risk fails constitutes having a contingency plan.
- Transfer. Transferring a risk involves making it somebody else's responsibility. For example, a risk owner might choose to purchase insurance against a potential loss.

There are many occasions in which more than one risk treatment option is selected. For example, a risk owner may chose to do less of something (reduction) and to also insure (transfer) the residual risk.

There is a lot of flexibility in how additional information about individual risks can be recorded. To make the risk information usable, the critical step is to capture the key information described above in a consistent way and to then share it through the appropriate list of risks, known as the ***risk register***.

<u>The Cyber Risk Register</u>

***risk register*** *– a central repository that contains entries for each potential, significant loss or damage exposure. Usually, there is a minimum* ***materiality*** *threshold; for example, a minimum potential financial loss value that must be met or exceeded before an entry in the repository is required. If a* ***risk*** *does occur, it technically becomes an issue (rather than a risk). Items can continue to be tracked within a risk register until the impact has been successfully managed and the root cause(s) have been resolved to the extent that the risk is not likely to occur again.*

Although a risk register is simply a list of risks, if it has key information about each risk captured using consistent formats, it can provide simple ways to identify:

- Similar or identical risks that are being reported.
- Risks that can combine (stacked risks) to create more overall potential problems for part of the security landscape than the individual risks suggest.
- The comparative risk priorities that should be addressed.

The important thing about a cyber risk register is that it captures any material risks that have the potential to cause significant harm or disruption to the digital landscape. That means anything that can substantially impact the cybersecurity ecosystem should be managed and monitored here.

Large organizations often mandate that different people manage different magnitudes of risk. This is completely okay, provided that there is a process to escalate risks above a clearly-defined materiality level up to the cybersecurity manager's attention.

In those circumstances, it is still better for everybody to use a single risk register and to simply restrict access to or visibility of the register, based on each person's privilege level. This will help to ensure that overall risk trends and patterns can be more easily identified and that escalated risks will already be recorded in a standard format.

Another reason for using a single risk register is to help identify stacked risks.

Remember, stacked risks occur when different individual risks can cumulatively impact part of an organization's digital landscape in unexpected ways. For example, there could be three separate risks, reported by three different departments in an organization, which all impact the same part of the attack surface or the same business process, application, or physical location. The only way a risk manager can make the connection and can report such patterns is if this information is recorded in the same place.

The more intelligently the method of capturing and managing a risk register is constructed, the more informed and effective risk managers will be at managing the cybersecurity priorities and keeping the organization safer from attack, intrusion or other failures.

As an example, an advanced cyber risk register will allow risk owners to select from multiple-choice lists of applications, critical business processes, assets, sites and other key parameters. This way, different risk managers can use those same variables to analyze patterns of risk against those parameters.

A cyber risk register is a reactive, ongoing operational mechanism that helps risk managers understand the overall risk position at any point in time.

The usefulness of the register depends on how conscientiously risk owners update it and how well engineered its risk information selections are.

A major benefit of a risk register is that because the materiality (impact and probability) and proximity of each risk has been documented, managers can make informed decisions about the priorities that need the greatest and fastest attention.

As useful as risk registers can be, it is not sufficient to solely depend on a reactive risk management technique. We will now look at what a risk assessment is and how it can be used to more proactively identify gaps.

## Risk Assessments

***risk assessment*** *– a systematic process for the proactive detection of potential hazards or gaps in an existing or planned activity,* ***asset****, service,* ***application, system*** *or product.*

Risk assessments are a proactive method of ensuring that risks are routinely analyzed and considered on any high-value targets.

Risk assessments are designed to identify any major risks that could harm a particular target that is under review. The questions they ask and information they capture depend on the type of target being assessed. For example, if I am performing a cyber risk assessment of an application, it is likely that my questions will be designed to help me understand if the application is accessible from the Internet, how many records it holds, if the information it transacts or stores contains personal or financial data, if it has the expected key security controls in place, if it has suffered problems or losses in the past, which technologies it uses, and so on.

This information helps me understand how attractive the application is as a target, how much damage might be caused if it is compromised and whether adequate security measures have been put in place.

Although risk assessment processes vary depending on what their target is, their objective is always to answer the same basic questions:

- How valuable and sensitive is the target?
- Have the right risks already been considered and addressed?
- What are the gaps (if any) that still need to be addressed?

A risk assessment should always be performed before something is put in service and at regular, defined intervals (for example, each time an update is issued or each year, whichever happens first).

Good cybersecurity practices ensure that risk assessments of target items critical to the digital landscape are performed. These target items specifically include:

- Technology services (internal or external).
- New hardware, especially network-attached devices.
- Software applications.
- New data exchange connections (inbound or outbound).
- Any data storage locations.
- Network access points and other gateways.
- ...

The results from risk assessments help actively understand the collection of risks that apply to particular processes or components that affect the cybersecurity position of an organization.

If a risk that surpasses an organization's materiality threshold is identified during an assessment, this should also be noted in the risk register.

These assessments help to drive a consistent, proactive approach to identifying risks as early as possible, when the risks are cheaper and easier to manage.

## How to Apply Risk-Based Cybersecurity Management

It is unlikely that many organizations can afford to adequately secure everything in their digital landscapes. This means that it is important to efficiently focus efforts on securing the items that create the highest business revenues or that, if compromised, would have the greatest impact on business earnings.

This is known as taking a **risk-based** approach because it uses the potential impact and value of each item being compromised to help determine its priority.

***risk-based*** *– an approach that considers the financial impact of a failure, along with its probability and proximity, to determine its comparative significance and priority for treatment.*

With limitations on budgets and resources, it is necessary to take a step-by-step approach to (i) understanding what the business's real priorities are, (ii) optimizing the environment to maximize the value and coverage the security will deliver, and (iii) delivering the appropriate security controls.

When trying to secure a new or previously non-secure environment, rather than attempting to secure everything on the first pass, a cybersecurity manager is likely to use a faster, risk-based approach to:

- Identify the highest-value information targets first.
- Identify the digital assets that information needs to flow through & onto.
- Verify the business case for how and where the information is needed.
- Consider the threats to the organization and the probability of them occurring.
- Minimize the footprint of any sensitive data, based on the business case.
- They can then efficiently add the appropriate security controls.

If there is a well-maintained, established risk register and set of risk assessment processes already in place, a new manager can use this information to help verify the priorities and implement actions with the right level of prioritization.

When risk capture and assessment processes are not yet implemented or mature, a new cybersecurity manager usually starts by running a high-level risk assessment of the organization. A simple version of that process is covered in the next chapter.

# 13. How Cyber Exposed Are You?

Having audited the 'in depth' security of many companies, I have seen that the gaps about which most enterprises need to be most concerned are the ones through which somebody could literally drive a truck.

One way of addressing these deficiencies is to use one of the available frameworks that provide logical, step-based guidance to gradually put all the correct controls in place. The NIST, COBIT, COSO, UK Cyber Essentials and other frameworks all have comparative strengths and overlap in their approaches to putting effective organization-wide approaches in place.

Although these frameworks all provide valid methods of assessing and addressing security gaps, there are some faster, easier ways to determine what an organization's current cybersecurity status is. You can probably answer these questions for any organization you have worked inside, even if you were nothing to do with their security department:

- Is employee and supplier security training mandatory and regular and does it include information about how easy it is to inadvertently bring malware into the company?
- Are employees unable to access organizational email on a personal device if it contains certain sensitive information or has been classified as 'confidential' or higher security?
- Do employees need to use more than 2 or 3 usernames and passwords to access the main business applications?
- Can employees plug devices other than those supplied by the organization into the main network (wireless or otherwise) without seeking permission?
- Do any key systems or applications fall over (have their availability disrupted) during weekdays?
- Do employees and contractors feel positive and supportive about their organization; is it generally considered to be a good place to work?
- Has the organization been kept safe from cybersecurity breaches or other losses of electronic data that attracted external attention in the past 12 months?

- Does security extend into the cloud services, mobile devices, supplier services, social media groups and other digital areas for which the organization is still legally responsible?

If you answered 'no' to two or more of the above questions, it is very likely that there are substantial cybersecurity gaps present in the organization you were thinking of. This is not an exhaustive test, but it does demonstrate that identifying whether an organization has significant cybersecurity vulnerabilities can be quite an easy task and require very little insider information.

Answers to these questions do not comprise sufficient evidence by themselves to present to the executive of an organization as a business case for investment in cybersecurity. Presenting a comprehensive argument for such an investment requires taking a more structured approach to create an understanding of the key business objectives and revenue sources, along with at least a basic cybersecurity analysis of the primary technologies and technology-related processes on which they depend.

In this chapter we will briefly explore how to identify the major symptoms of poor cybersecurity and how to translate them into a meaningful business case that helps to motivate approval for the correct investment to address them.

This is only a very basic framework that can be used as part of an organization-level risk assessment. It should only be used as a starting point.

I have applied these methods in many different companies and they always work. Often I had ten days or less to pull this information together. Taking a business-focused, risk-based approach to analyzing the major factors that impact an organization's cybersecurity makes it comparatively easy to capture and present a coherent overview of the current status.

The first and most important critical detail to understand is what the organization's main business and revenue-generating objectives are. This can be achieved by understanding which primary services or products the enterprise relies on, along with looking at the strategic intentions that define the organization's plans to move forward.

Unless this information is captured, it will be impossible to effectively inform key decision-makers about any gaps that were discovered. It is essential that any problems are presented in the context of their potential business impact. If they are presented purely as technical or procedural deficits, these decision-makers will usually ignore them.

For example, if I state that we really need to invest in $X for a security architect to help harmonize and reduce the size of our attack surface, a non-technical, executive decision-maker will not understand the relevance of this type of intangible concept.

If, however, I present the same issue in terms of the likelihood, cost, impact and disruption to business operations, customer access, and brand reputation, this makes it easier for this decision-maker to make an appropriate investment decision. My case will be even stronger if I include the additional business revenue benefits that may be achieved by improving the security architecture, since better security architecture can deliver a more trusted and robust customer experience by safeguarding data that is important to both the customer and the company. Presenting real examples and numbers that have a business focus is the only way to secure the necessary investment.

Understanding a company's business objectives and the value they create allows a cybersecurity professional to in turn understand whether existing defense-in-depth measures are adequate and ideal for the company.

The first item that should be assessed relates to cybersecurity governance. Remember, this means looking for the presence of a single point of accountability for cybersecurity management (one person) who sits on, or reports directly to the main executive board. Are all the policies and procedures relating to security under their control? Does their role require them to ensure that cybersecurity is consistently considered and managed during business operations?

I am not going to list all of the executive, policy and procedure requirements in this chapter, but the following governance questions can serve as a starting point:

- Is there a security steering committee? Does their remit include cybersecurity?
- Is there a regularly compiled cybersecurity status report? Does it cover all major defense-in-depth categories? Is it made available to appropriate managers?
- Are the cybersecurity department's responsibilities clearly defined? Are the primary disciplines within cybersecurity represented?
- Is there a cybersecurity policy?
- Is there an enterprise-level security architecture document?
- Does the security architecture go beyond the network into all areas in which the organization's information goes (cloud, mobile, ...)?

- Is there a security awareness training procedure and program? Does it include warnings about practices that can cause malware infections?
- Is there a risk management procedure (or system) that is maintained and that allows risks relating to data or electronic devices to be easily identified?
- Are there risk assessment processes in place for deploying new products, services and technologies? Do they include sufficient consideration of cybersecurity factors?
- ...

It is also important to check that any policy, procedure or training documents (if present) have been updated regularly and are actively sent to, read and followed by appropriate people.

The next step is to check if there are usable and accessible inventories of the key components of the attack surface. Specifically, this should include:

- Is there a single, centralized list of all primary applications that the organization uses? Does each application entry identify a business owner, number of users, the type(s) of information it manages (financial, personal, credit card, ...)?
- Is there a list of suppliers, both technology suppliers and other suppliers that may use technology on the organization's behalf?
- Is there an inventory of the digital devices for which the organization is accountable? Can the security status of these devices be checked; for example, to verify that the devices are running up-to-date software?
    - Does this include a list of 'approved,' secure device types?
    - Is the security configuration for approved devices documented and appropriate?
- Are all locations where electronic personal data for which the organization is accountable tracked and managed?
- ...

Keep in mind that having several systems in place to meet a single requirement creates gaps. For example, if there are four systems that track the application inventory, this is certain to be both inefficient and ineffective because personnel will not be able to query information about the applications in one place or to capture this information in exactly the same way.

Once the primary governance and management mechanisms that are (or are not) in place have been identified, it is possible to look at the organizational risk relative to each primary product or service.

For the purposes of a rapid risk assessment of an organization:

- If a company produces vast numbers of products and services, it's best to aim to evaluate the top five or ten; or,
- If these products and services rely on common systems, looking at them as product or service groups is the most practical way of evaluating and understanding the underlying business rationale and cybersecurity status.
- If there are large numbers of sites (physical locations) and data centers, evaluating a small representative sample of the sites is the best way to start.

Taking one primary product or service at a time, it's important to look at what they do (business objective), what electronic data they use, and, just like a plumber tracks water, to look at all the electronic locations onto or through which the information flows. This will provide an understanding of the potential points on the attack surface that warrant further investigation, what applications they rely on, the people (including suppliers) who operate them, and which procedures are in place to ensure that cybersecurity is consistently considered and applied.

Consider the type of data that each application uses. Does the application contain any information that must be subject to higher levels of security due to its sensitivity? If the data contains personal, financial or confidential information, the controls would reasonably be expected to be greater.

Only by understanding the type and amount of data and analyzing where it flows can you hope to identify where it could be compromised.

As an example, when examining a CRM (customer relationship manager) system, it was discovered that a full copy of the information was also being taken for analysis each week by another supplier. Had we only checked the main CRM application and provider, we would have found that the data was very well protected. By checking the other (unexpected) locations it was going to, we discovered some high priority security gaps and corrective actions!

At each location that is identified, all of the usual cybersecurity checks we have covered in this book should be considered. Does it have secure configuration, is it access controlled, is it monitored to ensure it is running up-to-date anti-malware, is the information correctly classified, is the device always promptly updated with patches from the manufacturer, and so on.

The procedural controls that govern these electronic locations should also be inspected. Are the staff members operating them required to regularly attend security awareness training classes? Are access privileges managed on the basis of providing the least amount of permission each person requires to do his or her job? Are administrative and operational roles separated?

A good organizational assessment of its overall cybersecurity status is like a good book: it has a beginning, middle and end.

At the beginning, you are looking to understand the business needs and focus, and then to determine whether all the headline items (governance policies, procedures and systems) are in place.

In the middle, a representative sample of key products and services are examined to understand which applications, people, supplier and digital devices they rely upon. This phase also involves seeking to understand whether the correct, major cybersecurity controls are in place at each step of the journey the business data follows.

As any gaps are identified, they should be recorded, along with the corrective action(s) that will address the problem(s).

At the end of this process, you will be able to pull together a report that summarizes the cybersecurity position that is (or is not) in place. Remember, an important element of such a report is a translation that explains how the gaps can potentially impact business revenues and operations.

When we started this chapter, we mentioned that when organizations suffer major breaches, they usually have substantial gaps. Although this kind of review may (also) identify very small problems, keep in mind that executives do not want or need these details; they need the headlines.

The assessment must be presented to an executive in the form of a summary of the major factors, along with an explanation of their potential business impact and the key corrective actions (and costs) that can fix them. The minute details should only be available for those who are interested.

Often, risks and gaps are not addressed simply because they were only presented as technical or procedural gaps. Unless such problems are presented in terms of their business revenue implications, they are unlikely to be addressed.

An example format for an executive report could include headline status for:

- Governance:
  - Cybersecurity executive management and escalation structures.
  - Cybersecurity reporting (including primary risks).
  - Cybersecurity policies and procedures status.
  - Cybersecurity architecture status.
  - Cybersecurity staffing.
- Operations:
  - All information assets (internal and external) are centrally inventoried and regularly assessed.
  - Places in which electronic information is stored have an information classification process that is followed.
  - Primary business applications and data storage locations are actively monitored
  - Identity and access is effectively and centrally managed.
  - Digital device inventories are maintained with security status.
  - Baseline security configurations are defined and followed.
  - Appropriate security requirements are embedded into the development and / or procurement of applications.
  - Effective Security Incident and Event Management (SIEM) processes are in place.
  - Attempts at network intrusions and malware infection rates are monitored, and any trends or peaks trigger appropriate alerts.
  - Patch management is timely and effective.
  - User privileges are set to the lowest possible level to facilitate work requirements.
  - Advanced firewalls are in operation.
  - An effective anti-malware solution is in place (and running on all expected devices)
  - Mobile device management is in place (and running on all expected devices)
  - Technical contingency plans (business continuity and disaster recovery plans) are in place for critical systems.
  - There is a data retention and archiving policy or procedure in place that ensures electronic information is not being retained without a business justification.

- Compliance:
    - A program of regular risk assessments is in place and tracks all key parts of the attack surface.
    - Penetration testing is being performed on Internet-facing applications before they go into use and before any update is applied.
    - A program of audits or assessments that includes checks against cybersecurity-related policies and procedures is effective and in place.

It is relatively easy to use these checklists to evaluate whether an organization has substantial and open risks that are likely to allow unauthorized access. The more difficult task is translating these gaps into business-related language that clearly highlights any probable business and revenue consequences from these deficiencies.

Poor cybersecurity is typically a symptom of the larger problem that a company's executive management is unaware of the issues and of the extreme personal and professional damage these issues can cause.

The items above are not an exhaustive list; they are designed to help perform a fast assessment of the major factors required to help manage the safety and security of the electronic data and devices that any organization relies upon to function.

# 14. What to Do When Things Go Wrong.

In this chapter, we cover:

- The difference between Security Events and Incidents
- Security Incident Management
- When to Escalate

You might notice that the chapter's heading states 'when' and not 'if' things go wrong.

It is statistically implausible to believe that any organization of any size will never have any form of intrusion, malware or other detrimental materials that affect its digital devices and require fixing. Despite this reality, some organizations choose to bury their collective heads in the sand, believing that denial is a potential solution.

According to a 2014 survey conducted by PWC for the UK Department of Business and Innovation Services, only 73% of large organizations acknowledged that they suffered from a virus or malware infection in the past year. So what really happened in the other 27%? Did they have great security practices or poor detection rates? Statistically, it is likely that they had poor detection rates.

Given the certainty that cybersecurity breaches will occur, it is essential for every enterprise to have something called a Security Incident Management process in place before things go wrong. Even organizations with only one security person need to have a playbook of instructions to follow when things happen.

Having a solid, reliable process for dealing with security incidents is vital to minimizing their cost and impact and to limiting the amount of time that the disruption lasts. The processes and capabilities required to clean up these events are known as Security Incident & Event Management, or SIEM.

Security Incident & Event Management (SIEM)

It is first useful to understand the difference between a ***security event*** and a ***security incident***.

**security event** – *a term used to describe a minor disruption to the* **digital landscape** *that is thought to be unintentional. Examples include a single failed* **device** *or a single user forgetting his or her password. Unusual patterns of security events can be an indicator of a* **security incident.**

**security incident** – *the intentional damage, theft and/or* **unauthorized access** *that has direct or indirect impact to any substantial part of an organization's information,* **systems, devices,** *services or products.*

Monitoring security events can provide useful information for developing security improvements. Security events are also an important source of intelligence for the security incident detection process.

Detecting and reporting incidents (violations or other intentional intrusions) is the first step in the security incident lifecycle.

Security incidents can cost a lot of money, significantly disrupt an organization's business operations, and create brand damage. Early and effective incident management helps to reduce the severity (time and costs) of this impact.

Effective security incident management requires that an appropriate process and team of incident responders with the necessary skills can be activated whenever something happens.

It is essential that this process is clearly defined and regularly tested by the incident response team. Without a well-prepared and tested security incident process, the cost and impact of any attack or other compromise will be substantially greater.

As part of a well-designed security incident management process, it is essential to ensure that the roles and responsibilities of the people involved in the process are clearly defined. This means not only defining the role of the security incident responders, but also any and all other roles that are critical to the process. If someone (like an outside consultant or a staff member from another internal team) is called on to help the security incident responders, they need clarity on their specific responsibilities before they can become useful.

The security incident process consists of five key lifecycle stages (six if you include the need to establish the process). These stages are best summarized as:

- Detection & reporting.
- Verification.
- Isolation (also known as quarantining).
- Cleaning (mitigation and restoration).
- Review (analysis of patterns and process deficiencies).

Some frameworks, including NIST, include descriptions of these stages as *detect, respond* and *recover.*

Detection and reporting

People within an organization need to know how to report any suspected or confirmed incident into the security incident process. Incidents should be able to be reported directly through manual channels.

Suspicious patterns or concentrations of security events should automatically trigger an incident event response.

Until an incident is reported and triggers the incident response process, the damage the violation is causing will continue.

As soon as a potential incident is reported, it has to be assigned an initial priority level. This priority level may change during an incident as additional information emerges.

Usually, the incident response process will offer a short list of 4 to 7 priority options. Each priority level needs to have definitive and easy-to-understand criteria. After all, there are some incidents in some organizations that are so severe they can cost millions of dollars per minute if they are left unfixed and others that turn out to have little to no financial impact at all.

The priority level selected for a particular incident is usually determined by the potential financial impact and/or the number of people and/or customers impacted, how badly affected they are and the sensitivity of the data or service involved.

If a security incident only affects ten people on a low-value system, the impact will be far less than if it were a business-critical system impacting hundreds, thousands or even millions of people. A low-value, low-user system can potentially be permitted to stay offline for a short time. Conversely, many businesses cannot afford for some systems to have any downtime at all. Think about airline or hotel reservation systems, or auction and property websites. Even a few seconds or minutes of interruption can result in huge financial losses.

When assigning a priority, it is also important to be careful to consider not only the immediate incident, but the wider implications. For example, if I have a malware infection on a small system, I may still need to assign it a priority category, if during the verification stage it is determined that the problem could quickly spread to much higher-value parts of the attack surface.

Clearly defined priorities will also help responders determine when a security incident needs to be escalated. Escalation to management can happen at any time during an incident, if it is expected to cause substantial business disruption or because the incident cannot be managed inside normal tolerances.

Setting a priority level will also define the target time permitted for each unfinished stage of the incident management to be completed. If the time allowed for one stage is exceeded, or the security incident manager is expecting the time to be exceeded, this should result in the incident being escalated and flagged as being in an ***alert status***.

***alert status*** *– an escalation flag that can be assigned to a security incident to indicate that it cannot be managed inside allowable time limits or other acceptable tolerances that are defined by an organization's security processes.*

Verification

Once a potential incident is reported into the process, a security incident responder (a role described in an earlier chapter) will need to verify whether the incident is real and, if so, to categorize it further.

As also covered earlier in the book, well-defined categories and multiple-choice lists can be used to help speed up the incident response process. This means that cybersecurity people should not only categorize the incident, but should also capture as much information as possible about the key parts of the organization (sites, services and products) and the attack surface (devices, systems, applications, data, network segments) that are involved.

The US Computer Emergency Response Team (US CERT) defines six categories for a security incident. These are:

1. Unauthorized Access.
2. Denial of Service.
3. Malicious Code (including malware).
4. Improper Usage.

5. Attempted Intrusion.
6. Investigation.

An organization's specific process may contain different labels for these categories. If an incident involves multiple categories, this will be important to capture and resolve.

The sixth category (investigation) is primarily a placeholder to indicate that the causes and effects of the incident are still being researched.

Back in chapter 8 (*Technical Cybersecurity*) we covered the typical lifecycle of a major cyber attack. We also previously discussed the fact that the earlier a problem is identified, the cheaper it is to fix. Although prevention is cheaper than incident management, it is also true that the earlier in an attack or intrusion lifecycle the problem is identified, the less it is likely to cost to fix. For that reason, a concept known as the **kill chain** is often used to help the incident team understand how far into the lifecycle the problem has been detected.

***kill chain*** *– a conceptual cyber defense model that uses the structure of* ***attack*** *as a model to build a cyber defense strategy. The stages in an* ***advanced persistent threat*** *are typically used as a framework, with cyber defense strategies (detect, deny, disrupt, degrade, deceive, contain) considered at each stage. The model works on the premise that the earlier in the lifecycle that an attack can be detected and defeated, the lower the cost incurred and damage will be. This model can be a useful adjunct to a defense strategy, but also has inherent gaps; for example, it works best for internal organizational* ***networks****, but is less effective when applied to information outside of a defended perimeter. The model does, however, very successfully emphasize that* ***cyber attacks*** *are much less expensive to deal with when they are identified earlier in the* ***cyber attack lifecycle****. This same model is also used during incident management to determine how far an attack has progressed, to help advise managers on probable costs and strategies to defeat it.*

The security incident responder is also likely to call in experts from relevant disciplines to help manage the incident. It is important that arrangements for adding these experts to the incident response team are agreed upon in advance to ensure that these individuals are available when needed.

Isolation (Quarantine)

If an incident is confirmed to have occurred, the affected components must be isolated to minimize the impact and prevent other parts of the digital landscape from being affected.

This can be a tricky step in the incident response process, since it is important to balance the organization's need to continue to function and provide services with the potential cost and impact of the violation.

Just as a surgeon must be careful to precisely limit the amount of body tissue he or she cuts, incident responders strive to precisely and carefully isolate the affected digital components to minimize system disruptions and to maximize the amount of organization-wide support for the incident response. Where network segmentation and redundant systems are in place, it is easier for the incident response team to reduce the level of business disruption.

If a disruption to operations is unavoidable, it's important to have well-defined communication and notification procedures already prepared, so that the people who rely on the affected systems or devices are immediately and concisely notified, with estimates of how long it will take to restore their services.

Managers of critical enterprise processes should be notified or consulted first whenever this is possible. A failure to promptly consult with affected managers can have unpleasant consequences for the security response team.

It should also be expected that security incidents will often be intentionally timed by any attackers to happen outside of normal operating hours.

Cleaning

Once the cause and affected components have been identified, the incident response team needs to be able to rapidly call upon people with specialized expertise to clean and restore these components.

In some cases, it may not be possible to immediately clean and restore a component to exactly the way it was. This makes it essential for the team to include, or to be able to urgently access, experts who are capable of identifying temporary workarounds that can put alternative solutions in place until the affected component can itself be fixed. Appropriate access to business continuity and disaster recovery plans are likely to be critical during this stage.

A further key consideration during the cleaning stage is to ensure the preservation of any evidence that may be required in future investigations. It may be necessary to involve digital forensics experts to capture all the requisite information to trace, prove culpability, or litigate against the attacker after the event.

Again, the criteria for when it is necessary to preserve evidence should be defined in the incident response process, though the incident response team may still require assistance or advice from digital forensics experts who could be on the company's staff or who work for outside consultants.

Review

As soon as the immediate incident has been resolved, it is always advisable to look further at what happened, both at the incident and process levels.

Such a review involves asking questions like: Is the incident likely to occur on other, similar components? Is it part of a larger pattern? Are there additional immediate steps that need to be taken to protect the digital landscape?

How did the process work? Was it effective? Did anything take too long? Were the roles and responsibilities adequately defined? Are there any lessons learned that need to be included as improvements to the process?

Any post-incident response review inevitably ends up analyzing whether or not the parts of the incident response process that define how security events and incidents are prioritized and escalated worked well or should be modified. This requires understanding which factors are considered in establishing these priorities and escalation criteria.

Since responding to security incidents is so important, having a comprehensive, well-designed and well-tested incident response process is critical to successful cybersecurity.

Equally important, it is essential to ensure that the people who play a role in an organization's functions are aware of how to report potential incidents to the correct department or individuals to trigger the security incident process.

Remember, it was reported that Target received an anti-malware alert before any of its customer data was taken. If that did indeed happen, and if the alert had triggered an appropriate incident response process, then potentially the data breach could have been prevented.

# 15. A Glimpse toward the Future

In the first full chapter we talked about how the technological rate of change is not only the fastest ever but is also accelerating.

It can be helpful for cybersecurity planning to understand how technology will continue to advance.

As our use of technology increases and matures, having a wider appreciation of the expected changes can greatly assist people in setting personal and professional cybersecurity strategies.

In this chapter we will look at trends and new technologies set to become more prevalent over the next decade and beyond. There is absolutely no certainty regarding how correct or incorrect these predictions will turn out to be. Many of the near-term predictions are, however, already emerging, or based on patterns that have continued for many decades.

The most amazing thing about technology is that we no longer need to consider *if* something is possible. It is now possible to create almost anything. Rather than considering whether or not something is feasible, the only real question now is – *'Will it make money?'*

The lure of profits, earnings and power will continue to be the main driving forces behind the advancement of technology.

We can begin with some easy predictions:

- The amount of electronic information will continue to grow rapidly.
- The costs for storing and processing electronic data will continue to drop.
- The amount of computer processing power will continue to grow in line with ***Moore's Law***.
- Display screens will become visually larger, more flexible and immersive.
- The number of devices we use that can connect to each other will grow.
- Technologies will continue to reduce in physical size requirements.
- Power sources (batteries included) will get physically smaller and will recharge faster.

***Moore's Law*** *– created in 1965 by Gordon E. Moore. It states that over the his-*

*tory of computing, the processing power of computers doubles approximately every two years.*

There is also a very important, underlying trend to consider. This concerns changes in the way in which companies earn profit.

Instead of selling one-off products or services, everybody is looking at how to create invaluable streams of services that produce regular income that derives from repeat business from the same customers. Items that were once one-off product purchases are increasingly becoming subscription services that guarantee ongoing revenues.

The closer any organization can get to their customers, the better they can learn how to extend sales of such services into new areas. This means 2 things:

1) Organizations want to increase the amount of information about their customers that they store and analyze.
2) These organizations want to use this customer information to turn items that are currently physical products into subscription services.

For example, instead of paying for a refrigerator and freezer, perhaps it will be offered for free as long as you sign up for a subscription to have essential products (milk, butter, cheese, ham, orange juice, ...) automatically supplied and delivered by a particular supermarket whenever you are running low on these items.

The agreement for the refrigerator will probably allow it to track those items, including how much is left, how much you use, when the products expire and almost certainly, which other items you also choose to have delivered. For added revenue opportunities, the subscription service will probably also include a display to promote other items in which it can be reasonably sure you will be interested.

It is also likely they will offer a lower subscription price if you agree that they can collect and sell information about you.

*Since I included this example in the first edition, these types of fridges became available; yet just a few years ago, many people believed they were still a long way off. Researchers agree that the speed with which we now adopt new technologies has been growing exponentially. When electricity was first discovered, it took many decades to become an available resource that was adopted in most homes. However, the first effective smartphone took only 3 or 4 years to be widely adopted by the masses.*

Putting electronics into anything that we possibly can is now referred to as the ***Internet of Things*** (IoT).

***Internet of Things* (IoT)*** *– the incorporation of electronics into everyday items sufficient to allow them to* ***network*** *(communicate) with other network-capable devices.*

There are home thermostats that can accept remote instructions to turn the heat up and down and can detect whether or not you are home. These devices can potentially communicate with other appliances to let them know if you are in or out; for example, the thermostat might communicate with the lighting system so it can switch your lights on in the evening as a deterrent against burglary, or might tell the dryer to function in economy mode because there is nobody home to urgently need the clothes.

Put simply, the Internet of Things is based on the idea that there is probably some value in anything electronic being able to connect to other electronic devices and to the Internet.

As things change, there will be early adopters, late adopters and frequent attempts at new technologies that are ridiculous and never succeed. Every year at the Consumer Electronics Show (CES) in Las Vegas, there are literally tens of thousands of new gadgets on display. Only a small number become successful.

With the price of technology power continuing to fall, more and more devices will be connected to the Internet. As we begin to carry, wear and house more connected devices we can expect that those devices will be targeted by all kinds of organizations and people, good and bad.

Wearable technology is also set to progress. Why put a computer in a jacket? Well, it could be useful if you could scan and change the fabric color whenever you want to or use the sleeve as a display for any messages that your phone receives.

One of the new gadgets just being launched includes a 3D food printer for your home. Put in some small ingredient cartridges, select your dessert, and the food printer will instantly make it for you. Simply print and serve. Having this device on the Internet of Things has the potential to allow it to download new recipes and also to monitor what you like most and to then suggest other things you might like.

We already have smart televisions that are fully functioning computers in their own right; in fact, in some ways they are more advanced. As I was writing the first edition of this book, one manufacturer issued a warning that conversations in front of their smart televisions could be recorded, automatically changed to text, and sent to the manufacturer to help with product improvement of their voice command services!

If you think that seeing targeted ads on your computer or tablet is disturbing, wait until those advertising display screens start displaying ads specifically for you as you walk past them. Imagine moving up an escalator on the subway and seeing the ads in front of you promoting the holiday you have been researching.

Another imminent profound change is the move toward something called ***augmented reality***.

***augmented reality*** *– the overlaying of a virtual digital layer of information onto a view of the real world. The digital layer may seem to interact with the real world, but the impact is limited to affecting the perspective of the user (or users) who are immersed in the experience. This differs from virtual reality, in which the immersed users can only perceive a fully artificial world. Advanced versions of augmented reality that can map and understand objects and surfaces, and can then seem to allow digital projections to interact with real-world objects, are referred to as* ***mixed reality****.*

In practical terms, augmented reality allows a person to wear a set of glasses that can project three-dimensional images into real space. You no longer need a screen on a smartphone or a monitor for a computer, or even a television screen in your lounge. Instead of all those (and other) physical tools, a person using augmented reality can summon an object of any size or shape, including large screens and three-dimensional projections, wherever they choose.

Using sensors, these augmented reality devices can also allow people to interact with those virtual objects. For example, a physician can call up a three dimensional medical image and manipulate it with his or her hands, making it larger or smaller, rotating it, even zooming in and examining different sections and angles.

Home users of augmented reality can see an object on a web page and then place a three-dimensional version in their real space to see how it would look.

In 2017, when I describe this, most people think the technology is years away from being available. Then they try a device, such as the Microsoft HoloLens, that is already available, and realize that this technology will be mainstream within just a few years.

Similarly, self-driving cars are set to revolutionize how we use transport. Most of us are not using our cars more than 95% of the time. Why have your own cars if you could order one to come immediately to your door? You could have it drop you off exactly where you want, with no need to worry about parking and maintenance costs. You can also enjoy a drink in the car if you choose. Rather than paying for and owning an entire car, you will literally be able to use one by the minute, hour and mile. Without the cost of a driver, this type of service, still reliant on technology, will probably be so cheap to use that it will soon cost little more than just the fuel for which you currently pay.

However, this also means that whichever car service you subscribe to will know where you go, when you go there, who and what you travel with, and more. Almost certainly, it will aim to show you targeted ads, or will offer you sponsored opportunities (stop here for 50% off your meal) during your journey.

You might think that self-driving cars will take a long time to catch on. However, self-driving technology has already proven to be 20 times safer (mile by mile) in terms of fatalities than humans driving. By 2020, most cities will already be supported by vast fleets of self-driving vehicles.

Health is also benefitting from technology advances. Many of us already use various devices to monitor our health, diagnose medical problems or improve our fitness. I already had my own life saved by a robot (a Da Vinci robot), operated by a surgeon, that was capable of access and minimally invasive techniques in an area of the body that the human hand alone was not capable of reaching.

However, health technologies are set to increasingly transform tests and procedures that currently require specialized medical facilities into lower cost, faster and safer options that will often be available at home. For example, there are now toilets that can analyze their contents on the way through and provide early alerts on a wide range of medical conditions from Diabetes to some forms of cancer.

And then there is ***nanotechnology***.

***nanotechnology*** *– incredibly small products and devices manufactured through the manipulation of items as small as atoms and molecules.*

From delivering non-invasive surgery, to enhancing battery performance, or even enhancing human strength and durability, the ability to manufacture, deliver and control technology at such extremely small sizes creates even more possibilities. Forget corrective eye surgery; in the not-too-distant future, you may be able to splash the right collection of nanotechnology on your eyes to get not only perfect vision, but also the ability to zoom in on distant objects, record what you see, or even overlay a computer display.

All of these advances also mean that far more electronic data about all of us will be created and will be accessible to increasing numbers of people and organizations.

Over the past 40 years, the progress in reducing the costs of storing information electronically and the physical size of storage, while increasing the speed of access, has been unbelievable. To put this into perspective, if you wanted to put the entire works of Shakespeare (text only) onto an electronic storage device, the electronic storage required (about 4 megabytes) would have cost around $4,000 in 1978. Today, you could store it for less than one cent.

The entire scanned contents of an average print library can already be stored on a few 2 Terabyte SD cards, no larger than your thumbnail.

Nobody ever thought that we would find a use for all that data storage capacity. They were wrong. As our ability to store content has become cheaper and easier, the depth of content has become greater. For example, the target for digital photography used to be 11 million pixels, as that was equivalent to the same quality that traditional photographs could achieve. Now digital cameras can exceed that resolution by a significant factor.

Our data storage demands are roughly doubling every 2 years. The speed with which we can access the information is also following a similar curve. If you think you have a lot of information to look after now, expect to be looking after at least ten times more information a decade from whenever you are reading this.

Collecting and using large amounts of data can give organizations a great deal of power. They can use it to better target customers, discover new revenue opportunities and identify areas in which to reduce costs.

The fact that more data volume and more types of data increase the surface area that needs to be protected also opens up new potential threats and exploits.

These changes mean we can expect attempts at data theft to become faster and more frequent. Attacks will no longer have to be conducted over a period of hours or days to be significant.

If you think back to the introduction and the humble smartphone application that you thought you downloaded for free, the payment really ranged from having the "generous" application vendor bombarding you with paid ads to pulling private information about you into their files, most probably for targeted marketing purposes as well.

The same pattern will become increasingly apparent through more and more mainstream practices relating to items on which we spend the most money, including health, food, transport, security and entertainment. You can expect more and more technologies to emerge that are designed to turn products into attractive, revenue-earning services that will (also) collect data.

In addition to expanding orders from customer groups, organizations also focus on reducing operating costs. Technology is thus also driven in this direction.

Voice recognition programs are becoming smarter and smarter. They are already starting to replace some voice call handling (call center) services. One advantage (other than cost) is that a computer voice system can communicate in almost any language.

It is doubtful that many call centers will have real people answering the phones ten years from now, and it is also likely that you soon may not know whether you are dealing with a person or a computer program.

If you have ever participated in an international phone or video conference with non-native English speakers, worry not. Within the next decade, it will be possible to hold a real-time conversation with someone even though neither of you speak the other person's language.

The speed at which technology is evolving also has certain effects on how quickly or slowly we choose to adopt it. Although televisions are evolving rapidly, few of us want to take on the cost of changing up to the latest features every 3 years. A similar situation exists with cars and with most household fixtures.

The technologies we adopt most quickly tend to be those that are consumable, cheap or offer substantial value beyond their cost.

If someone offered me a free smart refrigerator for a subscription, I might sign up, but if they want $500 for it, I would probably stick with what I have until it breaks down.

That means that we can expect wearable, consumable items to continue to evolve rapidly and higher-value items to evolve at a slower pace.

The phone I have in my pocket today will probably be embedded in my watch and in an invisible earpiece within a short time, but I probably will not be using a driverless car service for all my transport needs for quite a few years.

All these changes will affect the job market too. The demand to fill jobs, even those that require highly-skilled people, such as general doctors, will decrease as technologies become increasingly able to deliver faster, more effective and lower-cost alternatives. The need for doctors will certainly continue, but a medical condition will have to reach a certain point in the diagnostic and treatment phases before a person may need to be involved.

If we think about the near-term impact that changes in technology will create, there are going to be new and expanding challenges for cybersecurity. As a species, we evolve by trying out lots of options. Most fail; some succeed. The same is true with how we are moving forward with securing our technologies.

The technologies that become popular and have sufficient security and protection to be reliable will endure. Those that under-identify their markets and their security requirements will fall by the wayside.

One thing that will change in the coming years is that organizational security will become strengthened through this attrition process. Organizations whose cybersecurity is repeatedly compromised will lose customers, and organizations that evade large breaches will gain customers.

Since I wrote the first edition of this book, it has already happened that cyber attacks have also moved more toward targeting homes and private individuals (where security tends to be weakest). That will also create new cybersecurity markets.

To summarize what is likely to occur over the next decade, expect to be dealing with new technologies and devices all the time. Expect the amount of data and locations of the data to continue to increase.

Looking further into the future, many people wonder about artificial intelligence and a point in time known as the ***singularity***.

***singularity (the)*** *– the predicted point in time when artificial intelligence exceeds human intelligence.*

There are still a lot of unsolved problems that need to be addressed before artificial intelligence can become a reality. Before that time, what is likely to happen involves an increasing degree of convergence between people and technology.

People can already be given smart, artificial limbs, eyes and ears, often with electronics connecting to send or receive information from the human brain. This has been referred to as ***wet wiring***.

***wet wiring*** *- creating connections between the human nervous system and* ***digital devices.***

It will be possible (further out) to make electronic information accessible to the human brain. For example, if you are heading to Italy for a holiday, instead of talking through an external translation device, it might be fun to be able to understand and speak Italian by 'loading' the language into a device that your brain can directly access.

Although these technologies are much further out in the future, it is likely that people will increasingly experiment with converging technology with biology. After all, if you can have artificially-manufactured organs like the ones already being created at several medical centers, there are unlikely to be many limitations on where technology ends and biology begins. If the failing brain cells in an Alzheimer's patient were replaced with synthetic nanotechnology, would that change who the individual was?

This is a philosophical point that I could not hope to approach in this book.

For the purposes of our cybersecurity objectives, the main consideration is that the rate of change will continue. There will be more data, in more places, and more technology to consider and protect.

As the Greek philosopher Heraclitus once said, 'The only constant is change.'

When I can paint my walls with a nanotechnology that allows me to change their color whenever I want, I know that one day I may get home to find that my walls have been hacked and are displaying some really awful content.

# 16. Bringing it all Together

Would you drive around in a car that had absolutely no brakes?

Probably not, but people and organizations frequently engage in similar behaviors when they start using technologies for critical activities without adequately evaluating them for their risks and without putting appropriate defensive controls in place.

In some cases, people do not address these risks because they believe effective cybersecurity is nearly impossible to achieve.

**The reality is that it is very possible to achieve substantial protection.**

Unfortunately, the vast number and severity of cyber breaches reveal that few individuals and organizations are taking the necessary steps to achieve this protection. Day after day, there are new cyber attacks and breaches damaging organizations and individuals through:

- intrusions or disruptions to technologies
- theft or manipulation of electronic information (data)

Some of these attacks hit the headlines, and some may affect you or I; for example, if your credit card or password information is among the stolen data.

Successful attacks usually occur because the people and organizations using digital systems had little idea of how to manage the risks they were taking with their technologies and electronic information.

The purpose of cybersecurity is to use reasonable means to keep important technologies and data secure. Achieving this goal requires a structured approach that uses all of the key processes that have been covered in this book. It requires that key technologies and collections of data are identified, analyzed for inherent risks, and appropriately protected based on their value.

If you ran a large chain of stores, you might not be able to prevent all thefts, but you could take steps to ensure that thefts were minimized and that only a small amount of merchandise could be stolen in a single incident. The same is true with cybersecurity.

Every enterprise should expect (and plan) to encounter and manage successful intrusions. However, it is also critical to ensure that appropriate layers of defensive, detective and corrective measures reduce the likelihood and impact of those events.

Remember that cyber attackers have the same criminal motives that have driven criminal acts throughout history. There are (in reality) no new crimes; there are only new ways to enact these crimes.

And, just as crimes involving theft have historically been prevented with locks, guards, safety boxes, and security tags, there are also preventive measures to safeguard digital devices and data.

**<u>Most</u> cyber attacks can be prevented if the correct proactive steps are taken.**

If we look back at the different case studies, there is a clear pattern indicating that whenever an organization cannot or does not bring together a comprehensive, connected and informed view of its security status, chains of individual risks form and create ideal conditions for substantial cyber breaches.

The fact that many large organizations still do not have their security under control often comes to light after widely-publicized data breach or service outage events occur.

However, situations in which security improvements are driven by a security breach (reactive measures) reflect an undesirable, unsafe status for any organization or its executives. It is far better (and far less expensive) for the security framework to provide a proactive, connected and informed picture of the substantial business risks, along with effective, actionable solutions.

There is a correlation between a relaxed organizational view of security and the likelihood of suffering large cybersecurity breaches. For large organizations, the correlation approaches 1.0, which means these variables co-occur 100% of the time.

Understanding the risks and implementing appropriate proactive security are critical because substantial security breaches can result in (i) huge costs (ii) the end of many peoples' careers and (iii) the loss of substantial amounts of information.

The first step towards achieving appropriate protection is for an organization's decision-makers to be motivated to improve security. Once they have the motivation, they can:

- Understand the gaps
- Design the security
- Implement
- Repeat

The right comprehensive security controls are readily available for those who are motivated and ready to implement them.

However, the biggest threat to all of us is our typical human complacency. Our natural tendency is to look at individual components and to resist the difficulties inherent in pulling together a holistic, informed and connected view of our security position. But it is only by pulling together the big picture that we can understand which individual tasks, risks and actions are most important.

As we approach the end of the book, let's look back at what we have learned about the critical elements in an effective approach to cybersecurity.

- The most critical factor is to have executive (board level) support for the correct investment in security. This requires presenting the executive with evidence that facilitates a clear understanding of the size and scale of the organization's risk exposure.
    - It is important to prepare and present a business case that translates risk assessment information about the organization's vulnerabilities into language that conveys the potential business impact.
    - It is essential that the business case is aligned with and based on an understanding of the organization's primary goals and objectives.
    - Security must be presented in the context of its financial relevance to business operations and business goals to gain executive support.
- Security governance structures then need to be defined and put in place. This includes not only policies and procedures, but also instructions that govern how a security steering committee operates and what the criteria are for escalating processes, including incident and risk management processes, up to the executive level for attention.
- Ensure that there is a robust cybersecurity architecture defined and that it spans beyond the internal network to cover all locations where the enterprise information flows.
- The threatscape (threat landscape) should be considered early on in the planning stages. This includes answering questions about who might be

motivated to attack the organization. The security posture should reflect the attractiveness of the digital assets and an understanding of how motivated various hostile groups might be to target those assets.

- Digital assets should be prioritized, classified and inventoried based on their business value. For example, business owners should be required to classify their repositories of information to gain an understanding of which sets of data require the greatest amount of security control.
    - Creating the foundations of an effective defense requires identifying the main business-critical information assets and placing appropriate controls on the digital devices and communication channels through which they flow.
    - Each group of important information must have an identified business owner. Each owner must be able to access and use a simple process to classify the scale, sensitivity, criticality and potential business impact this information has. This requires capturing consistent information about the data's volume, confidentiality, integrity, availability, consent requirements, number of users, and business, financial, product and service dependency.
- After consulting business decision-makers, a cybersecurity team should remove or destroy data that has insignificant or low value. Most of the embarrassing data revealed during breaches was kept unintentionally and contained a risk value that surpassed its benefit. Who needs to keep 10 year's worth of emails? Lawyers advise clients that there is generally more to lose through excessive email retention than there is to gain.
- Perform appropriate and regular risk assessments on technology targets, including:
    - Applications.
    - Hardware devices.
    - Other data storage locations.
    - Network security.
    - Suppliers that provide services through their technology.
- Reduce the attack surface to the minimum appropriate size to meet the business' needs. This includes defining the security architecture for any sensitive assets and information.
    - Use a security architect to help simplify the range of cyber defense points.
    - Zone the attack surface into discrete segments that reflect the value and sensitivity of the information they transact. Apply the greatest security to the highest-value zones.

- Use up-to-date 'nextgen' anti-malware across all devices that carry, store or transact information.
- Put strong user access controls that work on the basis of providing people with the lowest amount of privilege they require to perform their role in place.
- Adopt a coherent, robust and manageable identity and access management strategy that will allow you to rapidly improve access controls from a single point.
- Patch all devices and operating systems promptly with the latest security updates from their manufacturers.
- Deploy other key technical countermeasures such as advanced firewalls with strong policies to critical locations.
- Make sure the security settings on all applications, systems and physical devices are set to an appropriately high level and remove all default accounts.
- But most importantly – remember that defense in depth requires a holistic view of security. Physical security, procedural controls and cultural conditions are key contributors to the most significant and successful attacks.

## Understanding the Organization's Purpose & Business Objectives.

The extreme dependency organizations now have on technology and the immediate costs for any significant breach are factors that are pushing cybersecurity into a top 3 consideration for CEOs everywhere. This is because organizations cannot function effectively if their key operational systems, or the data they contain, are compromised. The impact involves not only the immediate business disruption but also the legal, brand and recovery costs.

Effectively managing cybersecurity requires taking the time to understand how the business earns its income and how this translates into the products and services it delivers to customers. This will then allow the value, function and priority of the different components to be considered.

Each organization's situation and outlook is different. The precise approach to security will depend on many factors, including:

i) **The nature of the business.**
The greater the sensitivity of the products, services and information an organization provides, the more robust the security will need to

be. The higher the value of the electronic information or services, the more attractive it is as a target.

ii) **The size of the organization & its risk appetite.**
The larger an enterprise is, the more likely it is that its decision-makers understand the risks of omitting and the benefits of having a strong security posture. This is because large organizations cannot survive for long without appropriate security. Large organizations that do not invest in cybersecurity and experience repeated breaches are taken down or taken over. Smaller organizations tend to have larger risk appetites. This is because (i) their value and size has made them (in the past) less likely to be targeted (ii) they have less to lose if they fail and (iii) they have more to gain if they succeed by taking chances their larger competitors cannot afford to take.

iii) **The culture and history of an enterprise.**
Companies which foster strong loyalty and positive feelings in their staff are less likely to suffer from insider threats. However, if an enterprise has no history of any significant impact from a cyber attack, this can lead to executive complacency and a higher likelihood of large security gaps that will lead to a substantial future cyber breach. It is thus important for cybersecurity professionals to make executives aware of such complacency if it exists, since resistance to investment in security is always due to a failure to inform the executive of the business consequences of not addressing security issues.

As described in point i) above, the nature of an organization strongly influences its security risks and needs. This means (i) the more attractive the technologies are to intrusion + (ii) the greater the scale + (iii) the larger the security gaps = (iv) the more likely the organization is to suffer cyber attacks.

Payment card systems, intellectual property and services an organization makes available over the Internet are all examples of business practices that create high-value targets for cyber attackers. The more of these the enterprise has and the more records each system has, the stronger the security posture needs to be.

Whatever an organization's situation may be, it is important for cybersecurity professionals to understand it and to present the need for security investments based on the business requirements.

## Cybersecurity is a Discipline

There are still many organizational decision-makers who believe that one person can manage cybersecurity without support. This is not possible.

The subject contains too many diverse areas that are evolving too quickly to be managed and resourced by a single individual.

In addition, remember the Edward Snowden effect. If one person has too much trusted access or control, the organization is at risk.

Cybersecurity Managers, Cybersecurity Architects, Network Security Analysts, Penetration Testers, Security Incident Responders, and Firewall and Intrusion Detection Configuration personnel are all examples of the more than 30 diverse, specific roles and skill sets required to competently develop and enforce adequate cybersecurity measures in a single large organization. For many organizations, it can make sense to procure these skills as services from specialized security services companies rather than to employ someone. In the same way an organization may not have a dedicated electrician or plumber on site, it can engage services; for example, penetration testing or security audits, from external suppliers for specific tasks.

Effective cybersecurity requires a team approach. It also requires more knowledge than any one person can acquire and maintain.

## Defense in Depth

Most texts on cybersecurity focus exclusively on the technical and immediate procedural controls, including:

- User access controls
- Anti-malware
- Secure configuration
- Firewall, intrusion detection & prevention management tools
- Encryption
- Patch management
- Technical security architecture
- Active security monitoring alerts for patterns revealed by port scans and other indicators of compromise
- Penetration testing on all Internet-facing applications before use or upgrade
- ...

It is important to understand that although all of these measures are very important, other traditional security layers are also needed:

- Effective risk capture and management processes
- Security incident and event management
- Business continuity and disaster recovery readiness
- Physical security
- Security awareness training
- ...

All the technical, procedural, and human factors layers that can help safeguard information should be considered.

## Creating a Holistic, Informed and Connected View of Cybersecurity

The key to cybersecurity success is creating a comprehensive, connected and risk informed approach that is aligned to the business strategy and objectives set by the executive.

It is not as difficult as it may seem to create a comprehensive and connected view of security risks; in fact, there are plenty of frameworks and platforms available to help with this process. Further review of the ISACA COBIT and/or COSO frameworks would be a good place to start for guidance.

Similarly, platforms including AdaptiveGRC (the one I designed) offer an easy way to start with an off-the-shelf set of synchronized processes for further refinement. These frameworks allow cybersecurity managers to pull all the process, risk and remediation information into one synchronized data source for easier management and prioritization.

When insurers establish a cyber insurance policy price for an enterprise, their calculations will typically include consideration of these indicators:

- How many **vulnerabilities** does the organization have?
- How robust are its **defenses**?
- How attractive and potentially profitable are its digital **assets**?
- How motivated are the **attackers** to target the organization?

If an organization has an informed and accurate understanding of these factors, appropriate defenses and no history of large breaches, it is far less likely to be breached in the future, so the insurance rates are lower.

## In Conclusion

It should be evident that we are all increasingly reliant on digital technologies. They are now the foundation of almost every product and service we use, even those to which we entrust our safety and lives.

The trend to increasingly include these technologies in products and services is continuing at a rapid pace.

This fact makes it increasingly apparent that we cannot tackle cybersecurity purely by seeking to protect digital networks.

In particular, everyday products are being increasingly connected to the Internet. Already, over half of all data usage is through or on mobile devices. With the Internet of Things becoming more pervasive, more and more of the technologies we rely upon will be incorporated into an even more diverse set of device and communication types.

This will make effective security even more important.

Most cyber attacks used to focus on compromising organizations. But as organizations get better at protecting their digital assets, we have seen technologies used by individuals are now targeted more frequently. Most private individuals have atrociously inadequate security on their personal devices. In the future, we should expect home cybersecurity to become more sophisticated as attackers develop new ways to gain power and extract money by breaching peoples' home-based systems.

Right now, most organizations have inadequate security that can be compromised far too easily. This makes improving the protection of the digital assets and electronic data for which organizations are accountable a priority.

From the case studies, it should be evident that organizations that are compromised are consistently missing a comprehensive, connected and informed view of the risks they are taking.

Keeping on top of trends in attack patterns and changes in technology usage are also important:

- Mobile technology represents more than half of all data usage and is increasing.
- Expect new forms of malware to be able to bypass many defense layers, increasing reliance on having effective defense-in-depth.

- Actively monitor changes to external threats and improve defenses accordingly.

Cybersecurity is about protecting organizations and ultimately people by preventing damage or harm from their electronic devices being compromised.

Too much security can make an electronic environment unappealing or difficult for an organization's customers, suppliers and staff to use. But too little security can easily erode confidence in a brand or enterprise.

Technology is now the backbone of any enterprise. In the same way that we take logical steps for our personal protection, cybersecurity professionals and business owners must also take logical steps to protect the electronic data and digital devices that are critical to the operation and survival of the organizations they serve.

Without an ability to trust and rely on our key technologies, our organizations cannot continue to operate, deliver services, retain customers and deliver revenues or (for non-profit organizations) justify the agency's value and existence.

No cybersecurity can ever be 100% foolproof. (There is always an idiot out there who is smarter than you are!) However, using a defense-in-depth strategy that includes technical, procedural and physical controls, along with creating a connected view of the information assets, security controls, risks and gaps, can ensure that any problem can be minimized, isolated and managed.

# Cybersecurity to English Dictionary

*A fuller version of this section is available as a separate publication.*

*Cybersecurity terms used in the book and others that may be of use are included here.*

**acceptable use policy** - *a set of wording that describes an agreement between any user and the enterprise that owns the service,* **application** *or* **device** *being accessed. The agreement usually defines both the primary permitted and prohibited activities.*

**access controls** - *rules and techniques used to manage and restrict entry to or exit from a physical, virtual or digital area through the use of permissions. Permissions are usually assigned individually to a person, device or* **application** *service to ensure accountability and traceability of usage. The permissions can be secured using (i) physical tokens (something you have); for example a key card, (ii) secret information (something you know); such as a password or (iii) biometric information - using part of the human body such as a fingerprint or eye scan to gain access (something you are). See also* **multi-factor authentication.**

**Advanced Persistent Threats (APTs)** - *a term used to describe the tenacious and highly evolved set of tactics used by* **hackers** *to infiltrate* **networks** *through* **digital devices** *and to then leave malicious software in place for as long as possible. The* **cyber attack lifecycle** *usually involves the* **attacker** *performing research & reconnaissance, preparing the most effective* **attack** *tools, getting an initial foothold into the network or the target* **digital landscape**, *spreading the infection and adjusting the range of attack tools in place to then exploit the position to maximum advantage. The purpose can be to steal or corrupt an organization's digital* **data** *or to extort money from the organization and/or disrupt its operations, for financial gain, brand damage or other political purposes. This form of sophisticated attack becomes harder and more costly to resolve the further into the lifecycle the attackers are and the longer they have managed to already leave the malicious software in place. A goal with this* **threat** *type is for the intruder to remain (persist) undetected for as long as possible in order to maximize the opportunities presented by the intrusion - for example, to steal* **data** *over a long period of time. See also* **kill-chain.**

**adware** - *any computer program (software) designed to render adverts to an end user. This type of software can be considered a form of* **malware** *if (i) the advertising was not consented to by the user, (ii) it is made difficult to uninstall or remove, or (iii) it provides other covert malware functions.*

**air gap** - *to use some form of physical and electronic separation to ensure that activities in one area cannot impact or infect activities in another. Used in the context of* **cybersecurity** *to describe how sensitive or infected* **systems** *are physically and digitally isolated so they have no possibility of interacting with any other systems and* **networks**.

**alert status** - *an escalation flag that can be assigned to a security incident to indicate that it cannot be managed inside allowable time limits or other acceptable tolerances that are defined by an organization's security processes.*

**anti-malware** - *is a computer program designed to look for specific files and behaviors (***signatures***) that indicate the presence or the attempted installation of malicious software. If or when detected, the program seeks to isolate the* **attack** *(***quarantine** *or block the* **malware***), remove it, if it can, and also alert appropriate people to the attempt or to the presence of the malware. The program can be* **host-based** *(installed on* **devices** *that are directly used by people) or* **network-based** *(installed on* **gateway** *devices through which information is passed). Older forms of this software could detect only specific, pre-defined forms of malicious software using* **signature** *files. Newer forms use* **machine learning** *and make use of additional techniques including* **behavior monitoring**.

**anti-virus** - *predecessor of* **anti-malware** *software that was used before the nature and types of malicious software had diversified. This is a computer program designed to look for the presence or installation of specific files. If or when detected, the program seeks to isolate the* **attack** *(***quarantine** *or block the* **virus***), remove it, if it can, and also alert appropriate people to the attempt. A virus is only one form of* **malware**, *so the term anti-malware is considered to be more inclusive of other forms of malicious software. However, as people are more familiar with the term 'anti-virus,' this can sometimes be used to describe various types of anti-malware. See also* **anti-malware** *and* **virus**.

**application** - *a collection of functions and instructions in electronic format (a* **software program***) that resides across one or more* **digital devices**, *usually designed to create, modify, process, store, inspect and/or transmit specific types of* **data**. *For subversive applications, see* **malware**.

**assessments** - *the evaluation of a target (for example an* **application**, *service, or supplier) against specific goals, objectives or other criteria through the collection of information about it. Usually, this is achieved through an established and repeatable process that involves discussing or answering questions about the target's capabilities and approaches. The purpose is to understand how closely the target meets the intended criteria and to identify any gaps or deficiencies. An assessment is different than an* **audit** *because it does not necessarily check for evidence (proof) that the responses are genuine and does not need to be carried out by an objective third party. It can be considered that a security assessment is usually akin to a consultative audit that does not seek to catch out or disprove the evidence provided by the target being examined.*

**asset** - *any item (physical or digital) that has inherent value. For* **cybersecurity,** *information items that can be monetized (for example, intellectual property and sets of personal* **data**) *are regarded as high-value assets due to their potential resale or blackmail value.*

**attack** - *the occurrence of an unauthorized intrusion.*

**attack lifecycle** - *see* **cyber attack lifecycle.**

**attack surface** - *the sum of the potential exposure area that could be used to gain unauthorized entry to any part of a* **digital landscape.** *This area usually includes perimeter* **network** *hardware (such as* **firewalls**) *and* **web servers** *(hardware that hosts Internet-enabled* **applications**). *It can also include extended areas of the landscape such as external applications, supplier services and mobile* **devices** *that have permission to access information or services of value. See also* **cyber defense points.**

**audits** - *the use of one or more independent examiners (auditors) to check if a target product, service and/or location is meeting the specific required* **control** *standards. This form of inspection requires that individual controls are tested to confirm their suitability and consistent usage. The outcomes from this type of event, including any gaps discovered and corrective actions required, are always provided in a final report.*

**augmented reality** - *the overlaying of a virtual digital layer of information onto a view of the real world. The digital layer may seem to interact with the real world, but the impact is limited to affecting the perspective of the user (or users) who are immersed in the experience. This differs from* **virtual reality,** *in which the immersed users can only perceive a fully artificial world. Advanced versions of augmented reality that can map and understand objects and surfaces, and can then seem to allow digital projections to interact with real-world objects, are referred to as* **mixed reality**. *See also* **metaverse** *and* **mixed reality.**

**availability** - *the assignment of a value to a set of information to indicate how much disruption or outage the owner considers to be acceptable. Often this is expressed or translated into a scale of time.* **Data** *with the highest possible availability rating would be required to be readily accessible at all times (no downtime permitted), often through the use of a fully redundant failsafe. The value assigned to the information's availability is used by the owner of an* **application** *or service to set the* **recovery time objective.** *See also* **integrity** *- a different, but related term.*

**backdoor** - *a covert method of accessing software or a* **device** *that bypasses the normal authentication requirements.*

**backup** - *(i) the process of archiving a copy of something so that it can be restored following a disruption. (ii) having a redundant (secondary) capability to continue a process, service or* **application** *if the primary capability is disrupted.*

*__biometrics__ - the use of physical qualities and attributes as a form of identity __authentication__. Fingerprint scans, retina scans and facial recognition are all examples of biometrics. As fast as new biometric options are created, the means to defeat them often follow. For this reason, biometrics is usually used only as part of a __multi-factor authentication__.*

*__black-box penetration testing__ - is the term used to describe a situation in which no advance information about the technical details of a computer program has been made available to those who are checking it for __vulnerabilities__. Whomever is performing the __penetration testing__ is operating without any inside knowledge, so the term is used to indicate a lack of visibility inside the 'box' (program) that is being checked.*

*__black hat__ - a person who engages in attempts to gain __unauthorized access__ to one or more __digital devices__ with nefarious (criminal or unethical) objectives. A __hacker__ with unethical goals, or no perceived ethical goals.*

*__black-listing__ - (in the context of __cybersecurity__) means adding a specific file type, __URL__ or __data packet__ to a security defense program to prevent it from being directly accessed or used. For example, a website domain can be blocked using __firewall__ rules to ensure that no user can visit that website through customary means.*

*__bleeding edge__ - using inventions so new, they have the likelihood to cause damage to their population before they become stable and safe.*

*__Border Gateway Protocol (BGP)__ - is a standard format that different __systems__ on a __network__ can use to share and make decisions about the path (routing) for information being transmitted.*

*__bot__ - is a computer program designed to perform specific tasks. They are usually simple, small and designed to perform fast, repetitive tasks. When the purpose of the program conflicts with an organization's goals and needs, a bot can be considered to be a form of __malware__. See also __botnet__.*

*__bot herder__ - is a __hacker__ who uses automated techniques to seek vulnerable __networks__ and __systems__. The bot herder's initial goal is to install or find __bot__ programs that can be used to achieve a particular purpose. Once one or more bots are in place, the hacker can __control__ these programs to perform a larger objective of stealing, corrupting and/or disrupting information, __assets__ and services. See also __botnet__ and __Mirai__ (an example of a botnet).*

*__bot master__ - alternative naming convention for a __bot herder__.*

*__botnet__ - shortened version of ro__bot__ic __net__work. A connected set of programs designed to operate together over a __network__ (including the Internet) to achieve specific purposes. These purposes can be good or bad. Some programs of this type are used to help support Internet connections, while malicious uses include* taking **control** of some or all of a computer's functions to support large-scale service **attacks** (see **denial of service**). A botnet is sometimes referred to as a **zombie army**.

**breach notification procedure** - some types of information, when suspected or known to be lost or stolen, must, by law, be reported to one or more authorities within a defined time period. Usually, this type of regulation applies to personal information. The required notification time period varies, but is often within 24 hours after the known or suspected breach takes place. In addition to reporting the known or suspected loss to the authorities, the lead organization responsible for the information (referred to as the **data controller**) is also required to swiftly notify anyone who is affected, and later on, must submit (to appropriate regulators) a full root cause analysis and information about how the organization responded and fixed any issues that were identified. To meet these legal obligations, larger companies usually have a pre-defined breach notification procedure to ensure that the timelines are met. The fines for data breaches are usually increased or decreased based on the adequacy of the organization's breach and **incident response** management.

**brute force (attack)** - the use of a systematic approach that can quickly generate large volumes of possible methods to gain **unauthorized access** to a computer **system**. For example, an automated script can run through the large but finite number of possibilities to try to guess a given eight-character password in a matter of seconds. Computing speeds make brute force attempts to try millions of possibilities easy if other defenses are not present. A common defense against this type of attack is to detect and block more than a few attempts at guessing any security information.

**buffer overflow** - exceeding the region of electronic memory used to temporarily store **data** when it is being moved between locations. This process is used by some forms of **malware** to exploit an electronic target.

**Business Continuity Plan** - (abbreviation **BCP**) an operational document that describes how an organization can restore its critical products or services to its customers, should a substantial event that causes disruption to normal operations occur.

**BYOD** - acronym for **B**ring **Y**our **O**wn **D**evice, indicating that employees and other authorized people are allowed to bring some of their own **digital devices** into the workplace to use for some work purposes. Some security people also use this term for '**B**ring **Y**our **O**wn **D**isaster' due to the uncontrollable number of security variables that this practice introduces for any information allowed to flow onto or through personal devices.

**CAPA** - acronym meaning **c**orrective **a**ction **p**reventive **a**ction. See also **corrective and preventive action system**.

**Chief Information Security Officer (CISO)** - *a single point of accountability in any organization for ensuring that an appropriate framework for managing dangers and* **threats** *to electronic and physical information* **assets** *is operating and effective.*

**cipher** - *the use of a key to change information into a secret or hidden format.*

**CISO** - *see* **Chief Information Security Officer.**

**Clear-box penetration testing** - *see* **white-box penetration testing.**

**closed system** - *a collection of* **applications, systems** *and* **devices** *that only have the ability to communicate with each other. No connection to any component outside the known and trusted group is permitted.*

**cloud (the)** - *an umbrella term used to identify any technology service that uses software and equipment not physically managed or owned by the person or organization (customer) using it. This usually provides the advantage of on-demand scalability at lower cost. Examples include* **applications** *that are hosted online, online file storage areas, and even remote virtual computers. Using a cloud means the equipment managing the service is run by the cloud provider and not by the customer. But although the customer does not own the service, he or she is still accountable for the information that he or she chooses to store and process through it. Usually a* **cloud** *service is identified by an 'aaS' suffix. For example -* **SaaS** *(Software as a Service),* **IaaS** *(Infrastructure as a Service) and* **PaaS** *(Platform as a Service).*

**compliance** - *the process used to verify that* **governance** *items (***policies, procedures,** *regulations and more) are being followed, and to identify when they are not.* **Audits, assessments,** *and* **continuous monitoring** *can be used to identify and report compliance deficiencies. Any identified gaps are usually tracked and resolved through a* **corrective and preventive action system.**

**confidentiality** - *the assignment of a value to a set of information to indicate the level of secrecy and the access restrictions required to prevent unauthorized people from viewing it. A typical example of a confidentiality scale is: (i) Public Use (ii) Internal Use (iii) Confidential (iv) Strictly Confidential and (v) Restricted.*

**consent** - *when electronic personal information is involved, there are often legal constraints that govern how the* **data** *can be used and where the information can be viewed, stored, transmitted or otherwise processed. In these circumstances, permission is often required from each individual to specify what information can be collected, where it can be processed and for how long it will be retained. These permissions can be represented by a series of tags on individual records or on the full data set. The attributes that require explicit permission may include, but are not limited to, country of origin, permission for export, limitations of use, retention and notification requirements.*

**containerization** – *(i) the partitioning of software functions within a single* **device, system** *or* **network** *that is sufficient to isolate it from potential harm or from other unwanted interactions with other software in the same environment or device. (ii) the complete isolation of one technology from another. For networks, this is also referred to as* **network segmentation**.

**containment** – *a stage during an* **incident response** *when steps are taken to isolate a confirmed problem (for example a* **malware** *infection) to prevent the issue from spreading to other areas.*

**continuous monitoring** – *using technology to actively monitor the ongoing security of an* **application**, *web site or other electronic service. The purpose is to provide faster alerts when any significant infringements of security that create potential* **risks** *are detected. For example, continuous automated monitoring for* **port scanning** *can detect patterns that can indicate an imminent* **attack** *and alert the appropriate personnel.*

**control** – *(in the context of security and* **compliance***) a method of regulating something, often a process, technology or behavior, to achieve a desired outcome, usually resulting in the reduction of* **risk**. *Depending on how it is designed and used, any single control may be referred to as preventive, detective or corrective.*

**control modes** – *an umbrella term for preventive, detective and corrective methods of defense. Each of these methods represents a different time posture.* **Preventive controls** *are designed to stop an* **attack** *before it is successful,* **detective controls** *are designed to monitor and raise an alert* *during* *a potential compromise and* **corrective controls** *are the rectification of an issue* *after* *an event.*

**corrective control** – *(see also* **control***) a method of defense that is introduced as the reactive result of an observed deficiency in security. For example, the addition of greater* **network** *segmentation after an* **attack** *can be considered a corrective control.*

**Cross-Site Scripting** (*also known as* **XSS**) – *a security* **exploit** *that takes advantage of security design flaws in web-generated pages. If the dynamic pages from a legitimate site do not have very robust rules, users' machines can be exploited by a 3rd party to present false links or dialog boxes that appear to be from the legitimate site, but are not. A specific instance of an XSS* **vulnerability** *is known as an* **XSS hole**.

**cryptanalysis** – *the art of examining* **cipher***ed information to determine how to circumvent the technique that was used to encode or hide it; i.e. to analyze ciphers.*

**cryptocurrency** – *any digital currency that makes use of* **encryption** *to generate and secure confidence in the units that are traded. These forms of payment are usually decentralized and unregulated, and it is difficult to trace currency owners.*

*This makes cryptocurrency the main form of payment for* **cybercrime** *and* **ransomware.**

**cyber** - *for anything using this as a prefix, see* **digital device.**

**cyber attack** - *an aggressive or hostile action that leverages or targets* **digital devices.** *The intended damage is not limited to the digital (electronic) environment.*

**cyber attack lifecycle** - *a conceptual model of the sequential steps that are involved in a successful unauthorized intrusion or disruption into a* **digital landscape** *or* **digital device.** *There are a number of models currently available; an example of the most common steps found across the models are illustrated within the definition of* **advanced persistent threat.** *See also* **kill chain.**

**cyber defense points** - *the digital locations where* **cybersecurity controls** *could be added. Examples of such defense points include* **data, applications, systems, devices** *and* **networks.**

**cyber insecurity** - *suffering from a concern that weaknesses in your* **cybersecurity** *are going to cause you personal or professional harm.*

**cybersecurity** - *the protection of* **digital devices** *and their communication channels to keep them stable, dependable and reasonably safe from danger or* **threat.** *Usually the required protection level must be sufficient to prevent or address* **unauthorized access** *or intervention before it can lead to substantial personal, professional, organizational, financial and/or political harm. In the UK this term is used as 2 words -* **cyber security.**

**cybersecurity architecture** - *see* **security architecture.**

**cybersecurity control types** - *categories used to help organize the defenses against* **cyber attacks.** *Usually, these categories are (i) technical (ii) procedural (iii) physical and (iv)* **compliance** *(or legal/contractual). Each of the* **cyber defense points** *should have all of the* **cyber control types** *considered and in place as appropriate to the* **risks.**

**cyber warrior** - *a person who engages in attempts to gain* **unauthorized access** *to or seeks to disrupt* **digital devices, systems** *or* **networks** *for personal, political or religious reasons.*

**dark Internet** - *originally refers to publicly accessible electronic* **data** *content that is unreadable only because of its format or indexing. For example, a store of raw scientific data may be Internet accessible, but without indexing or context it is considered to be part of the dark Internet. This term is now sometimes used to mean content that is intentionally hidden, where the terms* **dark web** *or darknet would be more accurate.*

**dark web** - *websites that hide their server locations. Although publicly accessible, they are not registered on standard search engines, and the hidden server values make it extremely difficult to determine which organizations and people are behind these sites.*

**data** - *information stored in an electronic or digital format.*

**data breach notification procedure** - *see* **breach notification procedure.**

**data classification** - *the process of arranging sets of electronic information into categories based on their value, impact, required level of secrecy and other attributes. Typical attributes for this categorization process include* **confidentiality, integrity** *(the need for the information to be uncorrupted) and* **availability**. *See also* **information classification.**

**Data Loss Prevention (DLP)** - *this term can describe both (i) the technologies and (ii) the strategies used to help stop information from being taken out of an organization without the appropriate authorization. Software technologies can use heuristics (patterns that fit within certain rules) to recognize, alert and/or block* **data** *extraction activities on* **digital devices**. *For example, a DLP technology may prohibit specific types of file attachments from being sent out via Internet mail services. These technologies can also prevent or monitor many other attempts at removing or copying data. There are workarounds that can be used by skilled* **hackers** *to evade detection by these solutions, including* **encryption** *and fragmentation. Although these solutions are becoming an essential line of defense, the most secure environments aim to prevent any significant set of data from being available for export in the first place. For this reason, Data Loss Prevention is often thought of as the last line of defense (a final safety net if all other security* **controls** *have not been successful).* **Information Loss Prevention (ILP)** *is an alternative version of the same term.*

**DDoS** - *acronym for* **Distributed Denial of Service**. *See* **Denial of Service** *for definition.*

**decapitation** - *(in the context of* **malware**) *preventing any compromised* **device** *from being able to communicate, receive instruction, send information or spread malware to other devices. This can effectively render many forms of malware ineffective because it removes any command,* **control** *or theft benefit. This is often a stage during* **takedown** *or* **threat** *removal.*

**deep web** - *Internet content that cannot be seen by search engines. This includes not only* **dark web** *content but also harmless and general content that is not indexed or generally reachable; for example, personal databases and paid content.*

**default accounts** - *generic user and password permissions, often with administrative access that is provided as standard for some* **applications** *and hardware for use during initial setup.*

**defense by design** - *the process of ensuring that protective security measures are consistently included and embedded from the earliest requirements stage of any component in a* **digital landscape**. *Components of the digital landscape include* **digital devices**, *electronic information, software* **applications** *and communication channels.*

**defense in depth** - *the use of multiple layers of security techniques to help reduce the chance of a successful* **attack**. *The idea is that if one security technique fails or is bypassed, there are others that should address the attack. The latest (and correct) thinking on defense in depth is that security techniques must also consider people and operational factors (for example processes) and not just technology.*

**Denial of Service (DoS)** - *an* **attack** *designed to stop or disrupt peoples' use of organizations'* **systems**. *Usually, a particular section of an enterprise is targeted; for example, a specific* **network**, **system**, **digital device** *type or function. These attacks usually originate from, and are targeted at,* **devices** *accessible through the Internet. If the attack is from multiple source locations, it is referred to as a* **Distributed Denial of Service**, *or* **DDoS** *attack.*

**detective control** - *(see also* **control**) *a method of defense used to help identify items or issues that may occur but that are not being defeated or prevented by other means. For example, an* **intrusion detection system** *may identify and alert a new issue but may not have the means to defeat the problem without additional intervention.*

**devices** - *any hardware used to create, modify, process, store or transmit* **data**. *Computers, smartphones and* **USB** *drives are all examples of devices.*

**digital device** - *any electronic appliance that can create, modify, archive, retrieve or transmit information in an electronic format. Desktop computers, laptops, tablets, smartphones and Internet-connected home* **devices** *are all examples of digital devices.*

**digital forensics** - *a specialized field in which personnel help preserve, rebuild and recover electronic information and help investigate and uncover residual evidence after an* **attack**. *See also* **indicators of compromise**.

**digital landscape** - *the collection of* **digital devices** *and electronic information that is visible or accessible from a particular location.*

**Disaster Recovery Plan** - *see* **Technical Disaster Recovery Plan**.

**Distributed Denial of Service (DDoS)** - *see* **Denial of Service**.

**DLP** - *see* **Data Loss Prevention**.

**DoS** - *see* **Denial of Service**.

**doxxing** *(also* **doxing***) - publicly exposing personal information on the Internet. Thought to be based on an abbreviation of the word 'documenting.'*

**drive-by download** *- the unintended receipt of malicious software onto a* **device** *through an Internet page, electronic service or link. The victim is usually unaware that his or her actions permitted new malicious software to be pulled onto and installed into the* **digital device** *or* **network***.*

**dwell-time** *- in the context of* **cybersecurity** *- this refers to how long an intrusion or* **threat** *has been allowed to remain in place before being discovered and eliminated. The length of time between intrusion and detection is an indication of how successful an* **advanced persistent threat** *has been. Although the dwell-time is expected to fall as cybersecurity measures mature, the average time is often hundreds of days and can be years.*

**Dynamic Host Configuration Protocol (DHCP)** *- the standard method used on* **networks** *and the Internet to assign an address (***Internet Protocol***, or* **IP***) to any* **digital device** *to allow its communications to operate. This address is assigned by a server (host) each time an authorized digital device connects to it.*

**eavesdropping** *- covertly or secretly listening in on a communication.*

**employee-led cloud adoption** *- a form of shadow IT where people working for an organization take it upon themselves to start using Internet-based services without going through official routes for assessing and configuring the usage to a secure standard. See also* **BYOC***.*

**encryption** *- the act of encoding messages so that if they are intercepted by an unauthorized party, they cannot be read unless the encoding mechanism can be deciphered.*

**endpoint** *- any electronic device that can be used to store or process information. Laptops, smartphones and even smart watches are all examples of an endpoint.*

**ethical hacker** *- an alternative name for a* **penetration tester***.*

**ethical hacking** *- the process by which supportive (***white-hat***)* **penetration testing** *experts assist in finding security weaknesses and* **vulnerabilities***.*

**event** *- see* **security event***.*

**exfiltrate** *- to move something with a degree of secrecy sufficient to not be noticed. Used to describe moving stolen* **data** *through detection* **systems***.*

**exploit** *- to take advantage of a security* **vulnerability***. Well-known exploits are often given names. Falling victim to a known exploit with a name can be a sign of low security, such as poor* **patch management***.*

**fileless malware** - *is a form of malicious attack that seeks to remain hidden by using techniques that avoid placing artifacts (files) on the storage area of a* **digital device.** *Instead, the attack seeks opportunities to append itself to legitimate services that operate in the memory (the RAM) of the target device. If an attack does not make any detectable changes to the file storage area and an organization is only running older security technologies that are not monitoring the activity in the memory (the in-memory area), the attack can be very difficult to detect. This is because only legitimate and expected services may appear to be running.*

**file transfer protocol (FTP)** - *the standard method used to send and receive packages of information (files).* **SFTP,** *or* **secure file transfer protocol,** *is the secure variation of this method that is used to send and receive* **data** *through an* **encrypted** *connection. Even if data is sent through an encrypted connection, it will not itself be automatically encrypted.*

**firewall** - *is hardware (physical device) or software (computer program) used to monitor and protect inbound and outbound* **data** *(electronic information). It achieves this by applying a set of rules. These physical* **devices** *or computer programs are usually deployed, at a minimum, at the perimeter of each* **network** *access point. Software firewalls can also be deployed on devices to add further security. The rules applied within a firewall are known as the* **firewall policy.** *Advanced firewalls are often equipped with other defensive features typical of more* **unified threat management.**

**firewall policy** - *the rules applied within either a physical hardware* **device** *(a hardware* **firewall***) or* **software program** *(a software firewall) to allow or block specific types of inbound and outbound* **data** *traffic at the perimeter of a* **network** *or* **digital device.**

**forensics** - *see* **digital forensics.**

**governance** - *the methods used by any executive to keep his or her organization on track with the management's goals and within acceptable performance standards. This is usually achieved by establishing* **policies, procedures** *and* **controls** *that match the enterprise's vision, strategy and risk appetite.*

**governance, risk and compliance** - *a term to describe the interaction and interdependence between the activities that (i) control any organization (***governance***) (ii) verify and enforce those* **controls** *(***compliance***) and (iii) manage any substantial exposures to financial impact that emerge (***risk***), often due to gaps in (i) or (ii).*

**hacker** - *a person who engages in attempts to gain* **unauthorized access** *to one or more* **digital devices.** *Can be* **black hat** *(unethical) or* **white hat** *(ethical) hacker, depending on the person's intent.*

**hacktivism** - *an amalgamation of* **hacker** *and activism. Describes the act of seeking* **unauthorized access** *into any* **digital device** *or* **digital landscape** *to promote a* *social or political agenda. Usually the unauthorized access is used to cause destruction, disruption and/or publicity. Individuals participating in these acts are called* **hacktivists.**

**hacktivist** - *an amalgamation of the words* **hacker** *and activist.*

**honey network** - *the collective name for a cluster of* **honeypots** *that operate together to help form part of a* **network** *intrusion detection strategy.*

**honeypot** - *an electronic device or collection of* **data** *that is designed to trap would-be* **attackers** *by detecting, deflecting or otherwise counteracting their efforts. Designed to look like a real part of an enterprise's* **attack** *surface, the honeypot will contain nothing of real value to the attacker, but will contain tools to identify, isolate and trace any intrusion.*

**host-based** - *describes a situation in which something is installed immediately on the* **device** *it is protecting, servicing or subverting.*

**Host-based Intrusion Prevention Systems (HIPS)** - *a version of an* **intrusion prevention system** *that is installed directly onto the* **digital device** *it is protecting from exploitation. See also* **intrusion prevention system** *for a description of its purpose.*

**hyper text transfer protocol (HTTP)** - *is the standard method used to send information (files, pictures and other* **data***) over the world wide web.* **HTTPS** *or* **SHTTP** *is the secure version of this* **protocol** *that can be used when the information requires a secure connection. It is rumored that some organizations have already or may soon be able to break the security for https/shttp.*

**IAM** - *alternative version of the acronym for* **IDAM.** *See* **IDAM.**

**IDAM** - *acronym for* **Identity & Access Management.** *The collection of processes and technologies used to manage, confirm, monitor and control legitimate access to* **systems** *by authorized account. This includes measures to ensure each access request is from a verified, expected and legitimate person or entity.*

**identity and access controls** - *method(s) of regulating how each person and computer service is confirmed to be who they claim to be (authentication) and how their permissions are monitored. See also* **IDAM.**

**Identity & Access Management** - *see* **IDAM.**

**incident** - *see* **security incident.**

**incident response** - *a prepared set of processes that should be triggered when any known or suspected event takes place that could cause material damage to an organization. The typical stages are (i) verify the event is real and identify the affected areas, (ii) contain the problem (usually by isolating, disabling or disconnecting the affected pieces), (iii) understand and eradicate the root cause, (iv)* *restore the affected components to their fixed state and (v) review how the process went to identify improvements that should be made. An incident response may also be required to trigger other response* **procedures**, *such as a* **breach notification procedure**, *if there is any information which has been lost that is subject to a notification requirement. For example, the loss of any personal information beyond what might be found in a phone book entry is usually considered to be a notifiable event.*

**infection** - *(in the context of* **cybersecurity**), *unwanted invasion by an outside agent that an* **attacker** *uses to create damage or disruption.*

**information classification** - *the assignment of one or more values to a collection of knowledge that help us understand how alike it is to any other set of knowledge. For information security, this is usually achieved by assigning values against* **confidentiality**, **integrity** *and* **availability**, *or CIA. A fourth category,* **consent** *is also sometimes used where the set of knowledge includes information on private individuals. This assignment of categories can then be used to more easily select the security and recovery approach appropriate to the information value and impact.* **Data classification** *is a subset of information classification as it only includes electronic information, whereas information classification includes any form of information, including paper and other physical formats.*

**information systems** - see **systems**.

**inherent risk** - *the level of exposure to loss, or the impact something has, before any mitigating* **controls** *are taken into consideration. For example, holding credit card* **data** *in a* **system** *brings an inherent risk to the system. See also* **residual risk**.

**integrity** - *a value that can be assigned to a set of information to indicate how sensitive it is to degradation of accuracy (such as unauthorized modification) or* **data** *loss. Loss in this context is about losing information without the ability for anyone to recover it from the* **system** *it was entered into (it is not about theft). Often this value is expressed or translated into a scale of time. For example, data with the highest possible integrity rating could be given a value of 'no data loss permitted.' If it were permitted to lose up to 4 hours of data that had been processed, the value would be '4 hours.' Usually, if any data loss is permitted, it means that there will be other processes in place to address the loss of the electronic information. The integrity value assigned to any system or* **application** *is used to set the frequency that the information is subject to backup, or in very sensitive systems with no data loss permitted, establishes the need for a permanent secondary failover system.*

**Internet of Things (IoT)** - *the incorporation of electronics into everyday items sufficient to allow them to* **network** *(communicate) with other network-capable* **devices**. *For example, to include electronics in a home thermostat so that it can* *be operated and can share information over a network connection to a smartphone or other network-capable device.*

**Internet Protocol** *- is the set of rules used to send or receive information from or to a location on a* **network***, including information about the source, destination and route. Each electronic location (host) has a unique address (the* **IP address***) that is used to define the source and the destination.*

**Intrusion Detection and Prevention Systems (IDPS)** *- computer programs that monitor and inspect electronic communications that pass through them, with the purpose and ability (i) to block and log (record) key information about any known malicious or otherwise unwanted streams of information and (ii) to log and raise alerts about any other traffic that is suspected (but not confirmed) to be of a similar nature. These are usually placed in the communication path to allow the IDPS to prevent unwanted information from entering or leaving a* **network** *by dropping or blocking* **packets***. IDPS can also clean some electronic* **data** *to remove any unwanted or undesirable packet components.*

**Intrusion Detection Systems (IDS)** *- computer programs that monitor and inspect electronic communications that pass through them, with the purpose to detect, log (record) and raise alerts on any suspected malicious or otherwise unwanted streams of information. IDS are a variation of* **Intrusion Detection and Prevention Systems***, as they have no ability to block the activity; they only monitor, inspect and alert.*

**Intrusion Prevention Systems (IPS)** *- see* **Intrusion Detection and Prevention Systems***. A slight variation in IPS, compared to* **IDPS***, is that they may not collect any detection information and may only serve to block (prevent) unwanted traffic based on direct rules or instructions they receive.*

**keylogging** *- a form of malicious software that is used to record and disclose entries on a* **digital device***. This type of* **malware** *is often used to collect credit card details, user identities and passwords.*

**kill chain** *- a conceptual* **cyber** *defense model that uses the structure of* **attack** *as a model to build a cyber defense strategy. The stages in an* **advanced persistent threat** *are typically used as a framework, with cyber defense strategies (detect, deny, disrupt, degrade, deceive, contain) considered at each stage. The model works on the premise that the earlier in the lifecycle that an attack can be detected and defeated, the lower the cost incurred and damage will be. This model can be a useful adjunct to a defense strategy, but also has inherent gaps; for example, it works best for internal organizational* **networks***, but is less effective when applied to information outside of a defended perimeter. The model does, however, very successfully emphasize that* **cyber attacks** *are much less expensive to deal with when they are identified earlier in the* **cyber attack lifecycle***.*

***legal control*** *- (in the context of* ***cybersecurity****) the use of legislation to help promote and invest in positive security methods and also to deter, punish and correct infringements.*

***logic bomb*** *- a type of malicious software (****malware****) that only starts to operate when specific conditions are met. For example, if a particular date is reached.*

***log management*** *- the method of managing the significant volume of computer-generated files, such as event logs and* ***audit*** *trails, so that they are appropriately captured, collated, analyzed and archived.*

***malware*** *- shortened version of* ***mal****icious soft****ware****. A term used to describe disruptive, subversive or hostile programs that can be inserted onto a* ***digital device****. People can intentionally or unintentionally make these types of programs harmful. Intentionally-harmful versions are usually disguised or embedded in a file that looks harmless so the* ***attacker*** *who uses them can intentionally compromise a device. Malware that someone does not intend to be harmful can still disrupt a device or leak information; however, the harmful qualities can result from unintentionally poor construction quality, bad design or insecure configuration. There are many types of malware;* ***adware, botnets, computer viruses, ransomware, scareware, spyware, trojans*** *and* ***worms*** *are all examples of intentional malware.* ***Hackers*** *often use malware to mount* ***cybersecurity attacks****.*

***master boot record*** *- the first sector on any electronic* ***device*** *that defines which operating system should be loaded when it is initialized or re-started.*

***materiality*** *- to have a level of significance or magnitude to be of concern.*

***metamorphic malware*** *- a more sophisticated form of* ***malware*** *that changes all key parts of its code on each installation.* ***Polymorphic malware*** *uses fewer transformation techniques than this type of (metamorphic) malware does, as polymorphic malware usually only changes some key parts of its profile, but retains the same core virus.*

***Mobile Device Management (MDM)*** *- a technology used to securely control the operation and use of mobile* ***device****s such as tablets and smartphones. Able (for example) to remotely wipe information from a mobile device and control which* ***applications*** *and functions are permitted to be installed or run.*

***Moore's Law*** *- created in 1965 by Gordon E. Moore. It states that over the history of computing, the processing power of computers doubles approximately every two years.*

***multi-factor authentication*** *- using more than one form of proof to confirm the identity of a person or* ***device*** *attempting to request access. There are usually three different categories of* ***authentication*** *types: (i) something you know [often a password] (ii) something you have [perhaps a security token or access card] and*

*(iii) something you are [the use of* **biometrics***; for example fingerprint or facial recognition]. As an example, effective* **two-factor authentication** *would require that when access is being requested, proof would be required from at least two different categories.*

**nanotechnology** *- incredibly small products and* **devices** *manufactured through the manipulation of items as small as atoms and molecules.*

**NAS** *- acronym for* **network***-attached storage. A digital repository attached to a* **network** *where information can be stored.*

**network** *- a collective group of* **devices***, wiring and* **applications** *used to connect, carry, broadcast, monitor or safeguard* **data***. Networks can be physical (use material* **assets** *such as wiring) or virtual (use applications to create associations and connections between devices or applications). Usually, the devices on a network will have some form of trusted permissions that allow them to pass and share* **packets** *of electronic information.*

**network-based** *- describes a situation in which something is installed to protect, serve or subvert the community of* **devices***, wiring and* **applications** *used to connect, carry, broadcast, monitor or safeguard information (the* **network***).*

**Network-based Intrusion Prevention Systems (NIPS)** *- see* **Intrusion Prevention Systems***.*

**network segmentation** *- splitting a single collection of* **devices***, wiring and* **applications** *that connect, carry, broadcast, monitor or safeguard* **data** *into smaller sections. This allows for more discrete management of each section, allowing greater security to be applied in sections with the highest value, and also permitting smaller sections to be impacted in the event of a* **malware** *infection or other disruptive event.*

**OWASP** *- the* **O***pen* **W***eb* **A***pplication* **S***ecurity* **P***roject is an online community that aims to create free, public resources to help improve the security of software. For example, they maintain lists of the leading* **vulnerabilities** *and security* **controls***.*

**packet** *- (in the context of electronic communication) is a bundle of electronic information grouped together for transmission. The bundle usually includes control information to indicate the destination, source and type of content, and the content (user information) itself.*

**packet-filtering** *- passing or blocking bundles of electronic information inbound or outbound based on specific rules. For example, if a known* **threat** *uses a particular size, format and type of* **data** *package (***packet***), then a rule can be put in place, on either an advanced* **firewall** *or a similar device, to block content that matches those parameters from leaving or entering a* **network***. See also* **packet***. Also known as content filtering.*

***patch management*** *- a controlled process used to deploy critical, interim updates to software on* ***digital devices****. The release of a software 'patch' is usually in response to a critical flaw or gap that has been identified. Any failure to apply new interim software updates promptly can leave open security* ***vulnerabilities*** *in place. As a consequence, promptly applying these updates (patch management) is considered a critical component of maintaining effective* ***cybersecurity****.*

***penetration test*** *(also known as an* ***attack and penetration test*** *or* ***pen. test****) - checks and scans on any* ***application, system*** *or website to identify any potential security gaps (****vulnerabilities****) that could be* ***exploited****. Once the vulnerabilities are identified, this process then goes on to identify the extent to which these vulnerabilities could be leveraged in an* ***attack*** *(the penetration possibilities). Usually these checks are performed in a test area and emulate the same techniques that could be used by an* ***attacker****. This is to prevent any inadvertent operational disruption. The checks are typically conducted before any application or site is first used, and also on a periodic (repeating) basis; for example, each time the program is updated or every 6 months. Any significant gaps must be addressed (fixed) in a timeframe appropriate to the scale of the* ***risk****. Not to be confused with the term* ***vulnerability assessment****, which only identifies gaps without examining how they could be leveraged. See also* ***pivoting****.*

***penetration tester*** *- a person who performs simulated attempts at* ***attack*** *on a target* ***system*** *or* ***application*** *on behalf of the organization that owns or* ***controls*** *it. See also* ***penetration test*** *and* ***pivoting****.*

***persistence*** *- to seek continued existence despite opposition.*

***personally identifiable information (PII)*** *- any combination of information that can directly or indirectly distinguish (identify) who a specific individual is.*

***phantom vibration*** *- when you think you felt your smart* ***device*** *vibrate but find out that it did not, or when you realize that there is no smart device on that area of your body right now.*

***phishing*** *- using an electronic communication (for example email or instant messaging) that pretends to come from a legitimate source, in an attempt to get sensitive information (for example, a password or credit card number) from the recipient or to install* ***malware*** *on the recipient's* ***device****. The methods used in phishing have evolved so that the message can simply contain a link to an Internet location where malware is situated or can include an attachment (such as a PDF or Word document) that installs malware when opened. The malware can then be used to run any number of unauthorized functions, including stealing information from the device, replicating additional malware to other accessible locations, sharing the user screen and logging keyboard entries made by the user. Less complex forms of phishing can encourage the recipient to visit a fake but convincing version of a website and to disclose passwords or other details.*

**physical security** - *measures designed to deter, prevent, detect or alert unauthorized real-world access to a site or material item.*

**PII** - *see* **personally identifiable information.**

**pivoting** - *a method used by* **penetration testers** *and* **attackers** *to leverage a point of infiltration as a route for easier access to compromise, infect and/or* **attack** *other* **systems** *and* **networks.**

**policy** - *(i) a high-level statement of intent, often a short document, that provides guidance on the principles an organization follows. For example, a basic security policy document could describe the intention for an enterprise to ensure that all locations (physical and electronic) where information for which they are accountable must remain secure from any* **unauthorized access.** *A policy does not usually describe the explicit mechanisms or specific instructions that would be used to achieve or enforce the intentions it expresses; this would be described in a* **procedure.** *(ii) Alternatively, it can also be used to mean the settings (including security settings) inside a* **software program** *or operating system.*

**polymorphic malware** - *malicious software that can change its attributes to help avoid detection by* **anti-malware.** *This mutation process can be automated so that the function of the software continues, but the method of operation, location and other attributes may change. See also* **metamorphic malware.**

**port number** - *used as part of an electronic communication to denote the method of communication being used. This allows the* **packet** *to be directed to a program that will know what to do with it.*

**port scanning** - *a process, usually run by computer, to detect open access points (ports) that could be used to infiltrate or* **exfiltrate** *electronic information into or out of an enterprise.*

**preventive control** - *(see also* **control***) a method of security defense used to stop issues before they can become problematic. For example,* **multi-factor authentication** *assists in stopping* **unauthorized access** *from ever occurring and is therefore considered a preventive control.*

**privileged account** - *an electronic user access right that has elevated permissions to allow it to perform* **system, application,** *database or other* **digital landscape** *management functions. Usually, this form of access requires additional* **controls** *and supervision to ensure the elevated privileges are fully accountable and are not misused. Most forms of* **cyber attack** *seek to gain this form of access, as these types of accounts have control over their digital landscape.*

**privileged account management** - *the* **systems,** *technologies and processes used to monitor and* **control** *the activities of* **privileged accounts.**

**procedure** - *provides guidance or specific instruction on the process (method) that should be used to achieve an objective. Traditionally provided as a document available to appropriate personnel, but increasingly replaced by instructions that are built into computer* **systems** *to enforce the required steps. In a traditional quality model, procedures may reside under a* **policy** *as an explicit instruction for meeting a particular policy objective. See also* **policy** *definition (i).*

**procedural control** - *an instruction during a sequence of required steps to limit how something is or is not permitted to be used.*

**protocol** - *(in the context of electronic communications) is a set of established rules used to send information between different electronic locations. Protocols provide a standard that can be used to send or receive information in an expected and understandable format, including information about the source, destination and route. Examples of protocols include* **Internet protocol (IP), hyper text transfer protocol (HTTP), file transfer protocol (FTP), transmission control protocol (TCP), border gateway protocol (BGP)** *and* **dynamic host configuration protocol (DHCP)**.

**proxy server** - *is a program used to provide intermediate services between a requested transaction and its destination. Instead of sending the transaction 'as is,' it can adjust some of the information to help secure the anonymity of the sender. In addition, it may store (cache) any information that is accessed often to help speed up response times.*

**ransomware** - *a form of malicious software (***malware***) that prevents or restricts usage of one or more* **digital devices** *or* **applications** *or renders a collection of electronic* **data** *unreadable until a sum of money is paid.*

**red team** - *when testing for potential* **exploits** *affecting any critical or sensitive* **system**, *infrastructure or website, a team of* **penetration testers** *is usually used. This term is used to describe the group of penetration testers working together on this type of objective.*

**residual risk** - *refers to the remaining possibility of loss and impact after security* **controls** *(the* **risk** *response) for an item have been applied.*

**resilience** - *the ability to remain functional and capable in the face of* **threat** *or danger, or to return to function rapidly following any disruption.*

**risk** - *a situation involving exposure to significant impact or loss. In formal frameworks, risk can be quantified using probability (often expressed as a percentage) and impact (often expressed as a financial amount). Other parameters for risk can include proximity (how soon a potential risk may be encountered, and information about which* **assets**, *services, products and processes could be affected).*

***risk assessment*** *- a systematic process for the proactive detection of potential hazards or gaps in an existing or planned activity,* **asset***, service,* **application***,* **system** *or product.*

***risk-based*** *- an approach that considers the financial impact of a failure, along with its probability and proximity, to determine its comparative significance and priority for treatment.*

***risk register*** *- a central repository that contains entries for each potential, significant loss or damage exposure. Usually, there is a minimum* **materiality** *threshold; for example, a minimum potential financial loss value that must be met or exceeded before an entry in the repository is required. If a* **risk** *does occur, it technically becomes an issue (rather than a risk). Items can continue to be tracked within a risk register until the impact has been successfully managed and the root cause(s) have been resolved to the extent that the risk is not likely to occur again.*

***rogueware*** *- see* **scareware.**

***rootkit*** *- a set of software tools that can be used by* **attackers** *to gain privileged access and* **control** *of the core (root) of the target* **device***, where commands can be more easily run. Part of the function of a rootkit usually includes hiding malicious files and processes to help avoid detection and removal of the* **malware.**

***scareware*** *- malicious software that is designed to persuade people to buy an antidote for a computer infection. It usually masquerades as a commercial* **malware** *removal tool or* **anti-virus** *package, but in reality is provided by the* **attacker.**

***script bunny*** *- see* **script kiddies.**

***script kiddies*** *- an* **attacker** *with little to no coding (programming) or technical skills who makes use of available scripts, codes and packages to gain* **unauthorized access** *to* **digital devices, applications, systems** *and/or* **networks.** *Also known as* **script bunnies** *and* **skiddies.**

***secure configuration*** *- ensuring that when settings are applied to any item (***device** *or software), appropriate steps are always taken to ensure (i)* **default accounts** *are removed or disabled, (ii) shared accounts are not used and (iii) all protective and defensive* **controls** *in the item use the strongest appropriate setting(s).*

***secure file transfer protocol*** *(also known as* ***SFTP****) - see* **file transfer protocol (FTP).**

***secure hyper text transfer protocol (SHTTP)*** *- see* **hyper text transfer protocol.**

***security architecture*** *- a model designed to specify the features and* **controls** *across a* **digital landscape** *that help it to prevent, detect and control any attempts* *at disruption or* **unauthorized access.** *The model also ensures that all* **data** *exchanges are subject to appropriate standards sufficient to ensure that the data controller's chain of custody commitments are maintained.*

**security event** - *a term used to describe a minor disruption to the* **digital landscape** *that is thought to be unintentional. Examples include a single failed* **device** *or a single user forgetting his or her password. Unusual patterns of security events can be an indicator of a* **security incident.**

**security incident** - *the intentional damage, theft and/or* **unauthorized access** *that has direct or indirect impact to any substantial part of an organization's information,* **systems, devices,** *services or products.*

**Security Incident & Event Management** - *see* **SIEM.**

**security incident responder** - *a person who assists in the initial analysis and response to any known or suspected attempt at damage, interruption or* **unauthorized access** *to an organization's information* **systems** *or services.*

**shell** - *the user interface within the operating system of any* **digital device.** *Most* **cyber attackers** *seek to gain this privileged level of access to the devices they are attempting to subvert.*

**shell access** - *command-level permission to perform executive control over an electronic* **device.**

**SIEM** - *abbreviation for* **s***ecurity* **i***ncident and* **e***vent* **m***anagement. This is a name given to the process and team that will manage any form of minor or major interruption to an enterprise's* **digital landscape.**

**single point (of) accountability (SPA** *or* **SPOA)** - *the principle that all critical* **assets,** *processes and actions must have clear ownership and traceability to a single person. The rationale is that the absence of a defined, single owner is a frequent cause of process or asset protection failure. Shared ownership is regarded as a significant security gap due to the consistent demonstration that security flaws have an increased probability of persisting when more than one person is accountable.*

**signatures** - *(in the context of* **cybersecurity***) are the unique attributes - for example, file size, file extension,* **data** *usage patterns and method of operation - that identify a specific computer program. Traditional* **anti-malware** *and other security technologies can make use of this information to identify and manage some forms of rogue software or communications.*

**singularity (the)** - *the predicted point in time when artificial intelligence exceeds human intelligence.*

**skiddie** - *abbreviated form of* **script kiddie.**

**social engineering** - *The act of constructing relationships, friendships or other human interactions for the purpose of enticing the recipient to perform an action or reveal information. The individual(s) doing the social engineering use the victim's action or information for the hidden purpose of achieving a nefarious objective, such as acquiring intelligence about the security, location or* **vulnerability** *of* **assets**, *or even gaining the person's trust to open an Internet link or document that will result in a* **malware** *foothold being created.*

**software program** - see **application.**

**spear phishing** - *a more targeted form of* **phishing**. *This term describes the use of an electronic communication (for example, email or instant messaging) that targets a particular person or group of people (for example, employees at a location) and pretends to come from a legitimate source. In this case, the source may also pretend to be someone known and trusted to the recipient, in an attempt to obtain sensitive information (for example, a password or credit card number).*

**spoofing** - *concealing the true source of electronic information by impersonation or other means. Often used to bypass Internet security filters by pretending the source is from a trusted location.*

**spyware** - *a form of* **malware** *that covertly gathers and transmits information from the* **device** *on which it is installed.*

**SSL** - *is an acronym for* **S***ecure* **S***ockets* **L***ayer. This is a method (***protocol***) for providing* **encrypted** *communication between two points in a* **digital landscape.** *For example, this could be between a* **web server** *(the computer hosting a web service or web site) and a* **web browser** *(the program that a recipient uses to view the web page; for example, Internet Explorer). In the* **URL** *(the Internet address visible to the user), the use of SSL is denoted by an 'https:' prefix.*

**stacked risk** - *the phenomenon of allowing seemingly separate potential issues with potential impact (***risks***) affecting the same* **digital landscape** *to accumulate. Without adequate identification and resolution, individual risks can form a toxic accumulation of issues that can be leveraged together to create a risk substantially greater than the individual components suggest. Megabreaches are usually the result of stacked risk in combination with a motivated* **attacker.**

**stateful protocol analysis detection** - *is a method used by* **intrusion detection systems** *to identify malicious or unwanted communications. This method analyzes* **packets** *to determine if the source, destination, size and routing (***protocol***) is significantly different than its usual format.*

**statistical anomaly-based detection** - *is a method used by some* **intrusion detection systems** *to identify malicious or unwanted communications. The program reviews the metrics it collects to identify any groups of communication behaviors that are unusual or anomalous.*

***structured query language injection (SQL injection)*** *- a form of security* ***exploit*** *that takes advantage of security design flaws in web forms. Within some web pages, there are forms that users can complete. If a web form does not sufficiently validate (check) the content of the information returned to it, an* ***attacker*** *can create longer entries than expected that include commands that allow unauthorized and unexpected values into the database. The consequences can be the corruption of the database and transactions.*

***systems*** *- groups of* ***applications*** *that operate together to serve a more complex purpose.*

***takedown*** *- (i) the process of a defending organization rendering* ***malware*** *ineffective by removing its ability to perform its functions; for example, through* ***decapitation****. (ii) the process of an* ***attacker*** *making unavailable some or all of an organization's key* ***systems*** *or capabilities. (iii) to stop something from working.*

***technical control*** *- the use of an electronic or digital method to influence or command how something like a* ***digital device*** *can or cannot be used. For example, removing the ability to cut or paste information in a smartphone is an example of a technical control that can be used to minimize security* ***risks****.*

***Technical Disaster Recovery Plan*** *- an operational document that describes the exact process, people, information and* ***assets*** *required to put any electronic or digital* ***system*** *back in place within a timeline defined by the* ***business continuity plan****. If there are multiple business continuity plans that reference the same Technical Disaster Recovery Plan, the restoration time used must meet the shortest time specified in any of the documents.*

***threat*** *- any source of potential harm to the* ***digital landscape****.*

***threat actors*** *- an umbrella term to describe the collection of people and organizations that work to create* ***cyber attacks****. Examples of threat actors can include* ***cyber criminals, hacktivists*** *and nation states.*

***threat intelligence*** *- the collation of information about potential hostile actions that could occur, together with an understanding of their relative probabilities.*

***threat landscape*** *- see* ***threatscape****.*

***threatscape*** *- a term that amalgamates* ***threat*** *and land****scape****. An umbrella term to describe the overall, expected methods (****vectors****) and types of* ***cyber attackers*** *through or by which an organization or individual might expect to be attacked.*

***transmission control protocol (TCP)*** *- the standard method used for* ***networks****, including the Internet, to send and receive error-free* ***data*** *that retains the same order that was originally intended.*

***transport layer security (TLS)*** *- is a* ***cryptographic protocol*** *(set of rules) for allowing secure communication between two digital locations. It is the successor to the Secure Socket Layer protocol, but is often referred to as being an* ***SSL*** *protocol. It is a form of symmetrical encryption.*

***trojan*** *- an* ***application (software program)*** *that appears to be harmless, but that actually hides and facilitates the operation of other, unseen malicious and unauthorized software programs and activities.*

***two-factor authentication*** *- see* ***multi-factor authentication.***

***unauthorized access*** *- to gain entry without permission.*

***ungenious*** *- something that was intended to achieve one goal but has a spectacularly negative outcome instead.*

***Unified Threat Management (UTM)*** *- a security* ***device*** *that integrates a large number of security technologies and services. For example, a single* ***gateway*** *device that includes proxy* ***firewall, intrusion prevention****, gateway* ***anti-malware*** *and* ***VPN*** *functions.*

***URL*** *- acronym for* ***u****niform* ***r****esource* ***l****ocator. This is essentially the address (or path) where a particular destination can be found. For example, the main address for the Google website is the URL http://www.google.com*

***USB*** *- acronym for* ***U****niversal* ***S****erial* ***B****us. This is a standard connector that exists on most computers, smartphones, tablets and other physical electronic* ***devices*** *that allow other electronic devices to be connected. Used for attaching a range of devices including keyboards, mice, external displays, printers and external storage devices.*

***vector*** *- another word for 'method,' as in 'They used multiple vectors for the* ***attack.****'*

***virtual desktop*** *- a* ***virtual machine*** *that emulates the functions of a personal computer. See* ***virtual machine.***

***virtual machine*** *- a computer with an operating system that can run* ***applications*** *but that does not physically exist. Instead of running on an exclusive piece of physical hardware, the computer is merely a set of software and configuration files. Multiple virtual machines can exist on a single physical machine, or a single virtual machine can exist across multiple physical machines through the use of a hypervisor. Virtual machines are often used for security purposes, as they are quick to clean, easy to set up and useful for isolating* ***threats.***

***virtual private network (VPN)*** *- a method of providing a secure connection between two points over a public (or unsecure) infrastructure; for example, to set up* *a secure link between a remote company laptop in a hotel and the main company* **network***.*

**virus** *- a form of* **malware** *that spreads by infecting (attaching itself to) other files and that usually seeks opportunities to continue this pattern. Viruses are now less common than other forms of malware, but were the main type of malware in very early computing. For that reason, people often refer to something as a virus when it is technically another form of malware.*

**vulnerability** *- (in the context of* **cybersecurity***) a weakness, usually in design, implementation or operation of software (including operating systems), that could be compromised and result in damage or harm.*

**vulnerability assessment** *- the identification and classification of security gaps in a computer, software* **application, network** *or other section of a* **digital landscape***. This is usually a passive identification technique that aims only to identify the gaps, without exploring how those gaps could be used in an* **attack***. This should not be confused with a* **penetration test***, which may include information from a vulnerability assessment, but which will go on to explore how any vulnerabilities can be exploited.*

**water holing** *- a method of* **cyber attack** *that identifies a location where a group of targets are known to visit frequently for the purpose of infecting them with* **malware***.*

**web browser** *- the program a person uses on his or her* **device** *to view a web page. Examples of web browser programs include Internet Explorer and Firefox.*

**web server** *- is a computer that is used to host (provide) a web service or web site.*

**wet wiring** *- creating connections between the human nervous system and* **digital devices***.*

**white-box testing** *(also known as* **clear-box testing***) - is the term used to describe a situation in which the technical layout (or source code) of the computer program being tested has been made available for the security test. This makes the test easier and cheaper to perform, but usually results in the identification of more issues than* **black-box penetration testing** *does. White-box testing can start early in the software lifecycle before an* **application** *has ever been installed in any production environments, making security fixes substantially cheaper and easier to apply.*

**white-hat** *- a security specialist who breaks into* **systems** *or* **networks** *by invitation (and with permission) from the owner, using only ethical means and with the intent to identify any security gaps that need to be addressed.*

**white-listing** - *the restriction of 'allowed' Internet sites or* **data** *packages to an explicit list of verified sources. For example, an organization operating a white-listed* **firewall** *can decide to only permit its* **network** *users to navigate to a restricted and verified list of Internet websites. This is the opposite of* **black-listing.**

**white team** - *the people who act as referees during any* **ethical hacking** *exercise conducted between a* **red team** *and a blue team.*

**Wireless Intrusion Prevention Systems (WIPS)** - **devices** *that can be attached to a* **network** *to check the radio spectrum for rogue or other* **unauthorized access** *points, and to then take countermeasures to help close down the* **threat.**

**worm** - *a form of malicious software (***malware***) that seeks to find other locations to which it can replicate. This helps to both protect the malware from removal and to increase the area of the* **attack surface** *that is compromised.*

**XSS** - *see* **cross-site scripting.**

**XSS hole** - *see* **cross-site scripting.**

**zero-day** - *refers to the very first time a new type of* **exploit** *or new piece of* **malware** *is discovered. At that point in time, none of the* **anti-virus, anti-malware** *or other defenses may be set up to defend against the new form of exploit.*

**zombie army** - *see* **botnet.**

Made in the USA
Middletown, DE
20 September 2017